T0354689

Unveiling Grace

Unveiling Grace

A Journey Through Life
and a Walk with GOD

Shana Marie Burnett

iUniverse

UNVEILING GRACE
A JOURNEY THROUGH LIFE AND A WALK WITH GOD

iUniverse books may be ordered through booksellers or by contacting:

iUniverse
1663 Liberty Drive
Bloomington, IN 47403
www.iuniverse.com
844-349-9409

Because of the dynamic nature of the Internet, any web addresses or links contained in this book may have changed since publication and may no longer be valid. The views expressed in this work are solely those of the author and do not necessarily reflect the views of the publisher, and the publisher hereby disclaims any responsibility for them.

Any people depicted in stock imagery provided by Getty Images are models, and such images are being used for illustrative purposes only. Certain stock imagery © Getty Images.

ISBN: 978-1-6632-6745-0 (sc)
ISBN: 978-1-6632-6746-7 (hc)
ISBN: 978-1-6632-6747-4 (e)

Library of Congress Control Number: 2024921272

Print information available on the last page.

iUniverse rev. date: 10/16/2024

Contents

Foreword

It is often said that great minds discuss ideas, average minds discuss events, and small minds discuss people. Dr. Shana Burnett engages in discussions about ideas, events, and people while listening to help change the world into a place of emotional self-sufficiency and independence. Each word in every sentence that she writes to her audience is carefully chosen. It is her life story, with a clear purpose and intention. You may wonder how I can speak so confidently about the thoughts and actions of the author of this book. It is because of our personal and professional connections. I have confidence in my description of the author and her book because before she became known as Dr. Burnett, she was my friend, whom I called Shana. While I may not have been present for every moment of Shana's life journey, I have been privileged to witness many significant moments throughout her lifetime.

Unveiling Grace: A Journey Through Life and a Walk with God, as seen through my perspective, showcases Shana's ongoing transformation, influenced by the longstanding debate of nature versus nurture, which is guided by both innate characteristics and environmental influences. The nature versus nurture debate addresses how biology or upbringing shapes a person's traits. Nature represents inherent biological factors, such as genetics. On the other hand, nurture includes the effects of one's upbringing and life experiences on one's personality. Through my relationship with Shana, I have gained insight into her life and understand that she embodies nature and nurture. She is the unique product of genetic traits and life experiences.

Despite the many stages of evolution in Shana's life, she is, first and foremost, a mother. She imparts life lessons, love, and freedom to her children. Her maternal instincts have further enriched her natural aptitude for learning and teaching. Her dedication to education and learning extends beyond her family to the numerous students she has mentored, guided, and advised. She has used her innate and learned skills to elevate the awareness of those she has encountered. This is evident in her journey from being a hands-on educator to attaining a doctorate in educational philosophy and eventually becoming an author. She draws on her vulnerabilities to inspire others to embrace their weaknesses.

I had the privilege of accompanying Shana on her journey from receiving a master's degree to Dr. Shana Burnett. Her EdD degree reflects her ongoing educational experiences and how she applies them to her life. It also reinforces her dedication to talking the talk and walking the walk. I am confident that she engages in introspective conversations with herself to ensure that she is qualified to encourage others to take responsibility for their personal growth. Whether it is family, students, colleagues, or readers, Dr. Burnett's book offers insightful questions and practical solutions for personal and professional relationships.

Shana has accumulated many accomplishments throughout her journey, which she proudly wears as crowns. Her memoir provides a deep dive into her complex world of observational psychotherapy from two perspectives: her personal experiences at home and her professional experiences in her office. Her goal is to provide constructive solutions to the challenges of the world around her. Through *Unveiling Grace*, Shana demonstrates her storytelling prowess by exploring her human complexities and relating them to her audience.

—Sylvester L. Stephens, Author/Playwright

Foreword

As I was growing up, I quickly realized that life presents us with daily opportunities for learning and personal growth. It doesn't matter where these lessons come from or who teaches them; what truly counts is understanding their importance. My mother, the author of this book, always stressed that it doesn't matter how you start something but how you finish it. To that, the journey toward your goals is equally significant.

While many books offer guidance on striving to be the best version of yourself and experts provide valuable advice, the most influential life lessons I have learned did not come from a book but from my personal experiences. Watching those who came before me has been a unique gift, and I learned many lessons from my mother by observing how she handled challenging situations.

I vividly remember a conversation with my mom about the idea of perfection. As a young girl, I looked up to her and my dad as role models, expecting them to be flawless. It was a harsh realization to understand that they, like everyone else, were imperfect individuals doing their best to navigate life. They made mistakes, and I learned that titles like parent, teacher, role model, or mentor do not exempt anyone from imperfections.

Our life seemed perfect on the surface. We lived in an affluent suburban neighborhood, with my dad pursuing his dream of becoming a pastor. However, chaos was present behind closed doors. After my parents' divorce, our picture-perfect image shattered, and we had to leave the only home I had ever known.

Initially torn and confused, the chaos eventually led to clarity and peace. My mom played a crucial role in making decisions for our family behind the scenes. At first, I resented, questioning why one person had so much control. But soon enough, I realized that blaming her was not justified; she carried an immense burden of responsibility.

My mom, who is both intelligent and courageous, taught me that we do not have to face challenges alone. She is why I am the understanding and compassionate individual I am today. This book allows her to share her life experiences with the world; those who read it will discover valuable insights. I am grateful for her unwavering support of my decisions, even when they were questionable. I inherited a sense of freedom from her, and the lessons she passed on to me enabled me to carry them wherever life led me.

I am honored to present this book, which narrates my mother's life journey and her walk with God—a testament to her strength and resilience and the transformative power of love.

—Meiya Carter, Author/Student

About the Author

Dr. Shana Marie Burnett's story is one of grace, resilience, and transformation. Raised in the heart of Newark, New Jersey—a city known for its contrasts of challenge and triumph—Shana's life reflects both the struggles and the beauty that shaped her journey. Grounded in the values instilled by her late parents, Marie D. Burnett and Clyde H. Burnett, Shana embraced a deep commitment to education, leadership, and community empowerment. These pillars have formed the foundation of her life's work.

With over 30 years of experience, Shana has dedicated herself to the service of others. As an educator and leader, she has transformed schools, mentored countless young people and women, and led initiatives that have had a lasting impact on communities. Her expertise in education, leadership, and grant writing has brought resources and growth to schools and organizations in need of transformation.

In her groundbreaking book, *Transformative Leadership: Creating and Sustaining a Thriving School Culture*, Shana redefines what it means to lead with purpose and compassion. Her insights into building strong, positive educational environments have inspired educators nationwide. As Mayor Ras Baraka wrote in the foreword: *"Dr. Shana Burnett's dedication is a guiding light, urging us all to embrace the transformative power of leadership in pursuing excellence in education."* Her work has become a blueprint for leaders looking to create schools where both students and staff can thrive.

But Shana's greatest role is that of a mother. Her three children—Antonio, Meiya, and Julius—are the heart of her life, and their love inspires her every day. Parenthood has deepened her understanding of leadership, teaching her invaluable lessons in patience, empathy, and purpose. The balance she finds between personal and professional life has allowed her to lead with both strength and grace.

Shana's latest work, *Unveiling Grace: A Journey Through Life and a Walk with God*, is her most personal and courageous endeavor yet. This memoir, which took years for her to release, offers an intimate look at her journey through abuse, depression, divorce, and the grief of losing her parents. It's not just a story of survival—it's a story of triumph. Shana's hope is that her journey will help readers find the strength within themselves to overcome their own challenges, grow through adversity, and embrace the grace that lies in every hardship.

Beyond her career, Shana is a lifelong learner and adventurer. Her love for travel has broadened her perspective on the world, while her passion for the arts continually fuels her creativity. Shana also finds balance and healing in cycling and spiritual practices like Reiki, both of which help her maintain a sense of peace in a busy life.

Dr. Shana Marie Burnett's life is a powerful reminder that grace and transformation are possible for everyone, no matter how difficult the journey. Through her words, her work, and her personal story of resilience, she continues to inspire others to live with purpose, embrace their own transformations, and believe in the power of faith. Her story is a gift to those seeking light in the darkest moments and a call to action for everyone to discover the strength and grace that resides within.

Preface

A Tale of Resilience and Divine Dance

In the labyrinth of my existence, I discovered solace in the shadows. This book is more than just a story; it is an odyssey through the relentless storm of mental and emotional trials, a quest for sanctuary within the recesses of my mind, and an exploration of a relationship marked by profound complexities. Shaped by malevolent forces that swirled around my mother and me, love struggled to bloom, creating a distorted reality that only I could fully perceive.

Imagine retreating into the recesses of your thoughts, finding solace on a serene beach amid life's chaos. This metaphorical beach became my refuge, a place where, amid the tumultuous waves of my emotions, I sought answers. Guided by the sacred teachings of the Bible, I clung to verses like "Ask and it shall be given, seek and you shall find, knock and the door will be opened." These words, deeply rooted in my Catholic upbringing, became the light that illuminated my path through the darkest times.

In moments of desperation, I found myself on my knees, silently crying out within the confines of my mind. I poured my heart out to God, yearning for a sign, a confirmation of love's presence amid the chaos of my life. Despite my fervent pleas, the divine response seemed to echo only in the haunting silence.

This profound sense of abandonment left me questioning whether God, once my sanctuary of love, had turned away in my hour of need. Lost in the labyrinth of my suffering, I grappled with the purpose of enduring such pain, wondering if my gifts and talents were doomed to wither in the shadows of my existence.

Yet, through this relentless internal dialogue with God, I embarked on a transformative journey. It was within these shadows that I discovered the profound power of resilience, faith, and the untapped strength that lay dormant within me.

Unveiling Grace: A Journey Through Life and a Walk with God is more than a memoir; it is an invitation to explore these themes alongside me. This book includes a special workbook section designed to enhance your engagement with the material. Each chapter's exercises are crafted to help you apply the insights and reflections to your own life, fostering a deeper understanding and personal growth.

As you delve into this journey with me, I hope that the reflections and exercises will guide you toward your own revelations, allowing you to embrace the grace within yourself and navigate your path with renewed strength and purpose. This book is my testament to the power of overcoming adversity and finding divine grace even in the most challenging moments. May it serve as a beacon of hope and a source of inspiration for your own journey.

Acknowledgments

In the luminous embroidery of my life, I extend my deepest gratitude and love to those who have illuminated my path with unwavering support and inspiration. To my beloved parents, Clyde and Marie Burnett, whose enduring presence continues to watch over me from the celestial realm, your wisdom and love remain my guiding stars.

To my cherished children, Antonio, Meiya, and Julius, you are the beating heart of my existence and the source of boundless purpose in my journey as a mother. Your laughter, warmth, and unwavering belief in me have fueled my aspirations, and I dedicate this memoir to each of you, my precious gems.

In the symphony of life, I acknowledge the divine orchestrator, God, the Creator of all things. With profound gratitude, I recognize the omnipresent force that has been my guiding light through the intricate twists and turns of existence. In the pages of this memoir, I lay bare my soul, weaving the threads of my experiences, with profound appreciation for the divine guidance that has sculpted my narrative.

May this memoir stand as a testament to the profound impact of love, family, and faith, echoing the eternal connection with those who have shaped my story.

It's the going through that helps you get through.

Introduction

Unveiling the Tapestry of My Soul

The scars etched into the canvas of my past are more than mere remnants of time; they are profound imprints on the very fabric of my existence. Some of these marks are visible, healed with the passage of time, while others lurk in the shadows, dark and relentless, seeping into my soul and compelling me to grapple with their lingering presence. They shape my journey and define the contours of my being.

Imagine the grand stage of my life, where I often found myself cast in roles that felt both unjust and diminishing. Despite the divine potential bestowed upon me by God, the harsh realities of life sometimes overshadowed my sense of worth and purpose. Chilling memories, unexpected and unwelcome, have cast long shadows over my perception of love, happiness, and fulfillment. These shadows have left indelible marks on my journey, reminding me of the life I never wanted for my children.

Efforts to shield myself from the grip of social dysfunction, poverty, ignorance, and illiteracy inadvertently became chains that restrained my spiritual growth. These challenges marred my physical being and distorted my view of the world, making it seem as though the life God had envisioned for me was forever out of reach.

Yet, amid these trials, I held fast to a divine promise—a sacred assurance that God would guide me through the stormy seas of life. This promise became my shield, protecting me from being consumed by the tragedies that enveloped others. It is a promise extended to everyone, regardless of their past or future. Reflecting on my journey, I can now affirm with confidence that I am who I am because of the intricate dance between adversity and divine grace.

In the interplay of shadows and light, I have learned that adversity is not merely an obstacle but a bridge to uncovering our inner strength. It is in the darkest corners that the light of our resilience shines most brilliantly. Embracing these shadows has revealed the transformative power within me, guiding me through life's intricate dance. This journey, though fraught with challenges, has illuminated a path of growth, healing, and discovery.

As you embark on this journey through my story, I invite you to join me in navigating the delicate dance between hardship and grace. Let the lessons of resilience and faith light your path, revealing the untapped strength that resides within you. This book is not just a chronicle of my past but a beacon of hope and inspiration for anyone seeking to uncover their own inner light amid the shadows.

Welcome to the journey of unveiling grace.

Faith

- A Journey of Faith, Laughter, and Spiritual Awakening (Isaiah 40:8)
- Guided Through the Wilderness (Proverbs 3:5–6)
- Taming the Storm Within (Exodus 15:2)

A Journey of Faith, Laughter, and Spiritual Awakening

"THE GRASS WITHERS AND THE FLOWERS FALL, BUT THE WORD OF OUR God endures forever" (Isaiah 40:8). Imagine this: a Roman Catholic-raised only child, navigating the spiritual aisles of the supermarket of faith, sampling each offering with curiosity and wonder. That child? That's none other than me, and let me tell you, my journey of faith has been an exhilarating ride, brimming with unexpected twists, turns, and a whole lot of soul searching.

Growing up, I was firmly planted in the pews of the Roman Catholic church. Sundays meant donning my Sunday best, reciting prayers, and maybe sneaking a yawn or two during the sermon (sorry, Father). But as I grew older, I felt a tug, a curiosity to explore beyond the comfortable confines of my faith tradition.

So off I went, exploring the spiritual buffet of life. A Pentecostal church, where the energy was electric, and the congregation swayed to the rhythm of the Holy Spirit. Then, there was the Baptist church, where the choir's harmonies lifted me higher than a gospel tune on a Sunday morning. Next stop? I dipped my toes into the waters of the Masjid, where the call to prayer echoed through the halls, stirring something deep within me.

But wait, there's more! I found myself wandering into a Buddhist temple, where the air was thick with incense, and the sound of chanting filled the room with a sense of peace I'd never experienced before. And let's not forget the synagogue, where I marveled at the rich tapestry of Jewish traditions and teachings.

Through these experiences, I came to a realization: God cannot be contained within the walls of one religion. He's bigger than that, transcending labels and doctrines. My spiritual journey wasn't about adhering to one set of beliefs; it was about seeking truth, wherever it may be found.

And so I embraced a life of spirituality, weaving together the threads of wisdom I'd gathered from my diverse experiences. Isaiah 40:8 reminds us that while traditions may come and go, the essence of God remains constant, eternal, and ever present.

Life Lesson

Embrace the journey. Explore, question, and seek truth wherever it may lead you. Whether you find solace in the pews of a church, the halls of a mosque, or the quiet sanctuary of your own heart, know that God is there, waiting to meet you wherever you are. So go ahead and dive into the spiritual buffet of life. You never know what delicious truths you might discover along the way.

Guided Through the Wilderness

"Trust in the Lord with all your heart and lean not on your understanding; in all your ways submit to him, and he will make your paths straight" (Proverbs 3:5–6). All right, buckle up for the ride through the carnival of my life. Picture this: Proverbs kicks off my tale, telling me to let go of my navigational skills and trust God to be my GPS. The scars from my past? They're not just background noise; they're like graffiti on the walls of my soul, shouting, "I've been through some stuff!"

Life was like a boxing match where I squared off against my internal struggles and the heavyweight champion of external adversities. I ended up with a sense of ugliness draped over me, not the latest fashion trend, mind you, but a cloak others used to treat me like a poorly written soap opera character.

Instead of being a highlight reel of laughter and joy, my memories played out like a horror movie soundtrack. Painful echoes and indelible marks on the canvas of my existence, like a Netflix series I never signed up for.

Efforts to shield me from life's storms became chains, binding my spiritual growth and giving me more scars than a clumsy cat on a cactus. It was like trying to follow a recipe and ending up with a cake that looked like a tire.

Imagine my life symphony starting in a kindergarten classroom, innocent laughter echoing in the background, while beneath it all, a shadow lurked, just waiting to mess with the melody.

Have you ever been in a room full of people but felt lonelier than a sock without its pair? Or have you grappled with the weight of God's grand design for your existence? Welcome to my story, where the ink of my first experiences started writing a narrative destined to be everlasting. It's like a movie, with a clandestine kiss serving as an unexpected plot twist, foretelling the roller coaster of emotions and revelations ahead.

My childhood was a maze—the posh hallways of Catholic school intertwining with the gritty streets of the ghetto. It was like trying to mix oil and water. Add in the enigmatic riddles of my mother's character, the mysterious disappearances of my father, and relationships messier than spaghetti without a fork—it was a puzzle begging to be solved.

Balancing the polished day life and the gritty night streets, I straddled worlds like a tightrope walker with an occasional wobble. It laid the canvas for my quest for meaning, leading me through the labyrinth of identity. Questions about life's intricacies surfaced as I wandered through these corridors, like, "Why am I here? Did God accidentally drop me into this maze?"

In the wilderness of my existence, where the path was as clear as mud, Proverbs 3:5–6 became my survival guide. It was like God saying, "Hey, trust me. I've got a better GPS than you." And you know what? In the darkest moments, God's hand was the flashlight guiding me through the wild jungle of my life.

As my journey unfolded, I learned to trust in God's guidance. The scars that once seemed like fortress walls started crumbling, revealing a light that had been playing hide-and-seek. Once a deserted island of isolation, the wilderness transformed into a sacred space where I could have heart-to-heart chats with the Creator. Surrendering to His wisdom, the path became straighter than a freshly ironed shirt, leading me to a deeper understanding of my purpose.

As the echoes of Proverbs rang through the labyrinth of my life, I found solace in the assurance that my tumultuous journey was being directed by a divine hand. Instead of a haunted house of despair, the wilderness became the playground where my faith blossomed, and my identity was woven into God's grand design.

Life Lesson

Trust God's GPS, even when you think you know a shortcut.

Taming the Storm Within

"The Lord is my strength and my song; he has become my salvation. He is my God, and I will praise him, my father's God, and I will exalt him" (Exodus 15:2). In the grand symphony of my life, this section is like a powerful movement, blending the strains of relentless pressure, shattered illusions, and the wild escapade of breaking free from the chains of societal expectations. It's a bit like my personal remix of Exodus 15:2, where I turn life's storms into a divine jam session.

As the pages flip, we peel back the layers of my life's screenplay, and guess what? The grand plan we thought was foolproof is like trying to fit a giraffe into a Mini Cooper. Societal expectations are not the neatly paved roads we imagined but more like a twisted maze that's eerily good at hiding the exit.

In the vast landscape of my roller-coaster journey, where friendships were scarcer than a needle in a haystack, I strolled through a terrain marked by silent struggles. Picture it: the shades of friendships were more like a delicate spider's web, fragile yet holding significance beyond the surface. This section unfolds like a movie scene, and right in the middle, loss enters, stealing the spotlight.

Enter a devastating house fire, not just taking our belongings but snatching away a little friend's life. Imagine my mother, carrying the weight of grief in her eyes, breaking the news like a somber messenger in a Shakespearean tragedy. The world crumbled, and the air felt heavy with the weight of our loss.

Sitting in a miniature chair at school, enveloped by the repercussions of a world irreversibly altered, I received the devastating news—everything, including my friend, was gone as a result of the fire. The grief descended like a blow to the stomach, and I could almost envision a future devoid of the cheerful laughter of my beloved friend, now merely a recollection.

Our belongings turned to ashes, and the question hung in the air like a dramatic plot twist—what now? It wasn't just about losing stuff; it was about facing the vulnerability and displacement that came with such a catastrophic event.

In the aftermath, the journey to rebuild was a lesson in resilience. This section became a crucible, the flames of adversity forging a determination to rise above. Taming the storm required facing external challenges and battling the internal turmoil stirred by the profound impact of loss.

As the fiery trial cooled, a seed of strength sprouted within me. The loss became a poignant reminder of life's fragility and the resilience needed to navigate its unpredictable twists. I found the latent power to withstand life's storms through the ashes. The journey toward healing and empowerment began, fueled by the memory of laughter now echoing in the corridors of my soul.

The intricate web of loss and pain became the haunting backdrop of my life—a recurring theme reaching its peak with a fire that not only devoured possessions but left behind the charred remnants of displacement. Yet, in the ashes, a haven emerged—the unexpected refuge of a convent, where nuns became guardians of my transient peace.

Living within those convent walls briefly was like stumbling upon an oasis. In the chaos, simplicity and gratitude became my companions.

Shared moments of prayer and the rhythmic dance of communal meals, they soothed a soul battered by life's storms. With their silent wisdom, the nuns became beacons of hope in a narrative of loss and upheaval.

In the crucible of life's storm, where the winds threatened to extinguish the flame within, the hallowed walls of the convent became my classroom for taming the storm. This unexpected sanctuary became a testament to the resilience of the human spirit—a spirit learning to navigate chaos and emerge stronger.

As I uncover unforeseen reservoirs of strength and wisdom in the most unexpected corners, I am reminded of the universal truth that even amid the darkest tempests, a guiding light beckons us toward resilience and rejuvenation. Just as the melodious verses of Exodus 15:2 proclaim the Lord as our stronghold and deliverance, my journey serves as a testament to the transformative potency of faith and the latent fortitude residing within each of us—a voyage of mastering the tempest within and embracing the serenity that follows the storm's fury.

Life Lesson

Even amid the fiercest storms, an untapped reservoir of inner strength awaits its moment to shine.

Faith Notes

Enter the realm of spiritual exploration with open arms, anchoring your faith securely in the timeless truths of Isaiah 40:8. Here, within the sacred verses of scripture, lies a map for your journey—a journey that invites you to delve into the depths of your soul and to unearth the profound mysteries of faith.

Embark on this voyage with a spirit of curiosity and courage, unafraid to question and probe the boundaries of your beliefs. Whether you find yourself within the hallowed halls of churches, mosques, or in the quiet sanctuary of your own heart, know that God's presence is ever near, guiding your steps along the path of enlightenment.

As you navigate the twists and turns of life's spiritual terrain, heed the call to explore the vast buffet of spiritual wisdom that surrounds you. For within the sacred texts and teachings, as well as in the whispers of your intuition, lie hidden treasures waiting to be discovered.

Reflect on the timeless truths echoed in the pages of Proverbs, where divine guidance illuminates even the darkest corners of despair, transforming adversity into opportunities for spiritual growth. Embrace the intertwined journey of faith and identity, trusting in God's wisdom and resisting the allure of shortcuts along the way.

In the midst of life's fiercest storms, remember the promise of Exodus 15:2—that the Lord is our refuge and strength, a beacon of hope amid the tempest. Allow this truth to fortify your spirit, revealing the transformative power of faith to weather life's wildest challenges and emerge stronger and more resilient than before.

_____

_____

_____

_____

_____

_____

_____

_____

_____

_____

_____

_____

_____

_____

Workbook Section

- Prompt: As you journey through life's intricate pathways, do you rely on faith to guide you through unexplored territories, or do you find comfort in sticking to familiar routes? When faced with uncertainty and doubt, do you seek solace in divine wisdom, or are you tempted by quick fixes and easy solutions? In the midst of life's storms, do you tap into the inner strength provided by your faith, or do you struggle under the weight of adversity? Where do you currently find yourself on your spiritual journey?

Actionable Steps

1. Self-Assessment
    -   Reflect: Write down your current understanding and practice of faith. What role does faith play in your daily life? Are you more inclined to trust in divine guidance, or do you lean on familiar, safe choices?
    -   Evaluate: Think about recent challenges you've faced. Did you turn to your faith for strength and guidance? If not, what alternative paths did you take?

2. Journaling Exercise
    -   Explore: Describe a time when you were at a crossroads in life. How did faith influence your decision? What was the outcome, and how did it shape your spiritual journey?
    -   Contemplate: Consider moments of doubt or uncertainty. What has prevented you from fully trusting in your faith? How can you overcome these barriers?

3. Faith in Action
    -   Commit: Identify one area of your life where you can actively practice your faith. This could be through prayer, meditation, or stepping out in faith in a situation that feels uncertain.

- Act: Take a small but meaningful step this week that requires you to trust in divine guidance rather than relying solely on your own understanding.

4. Guided Prayer or Meditation
   - Focus: Spend time each day in prayer or meditation, asking for the strength to lean into your faith during life's challenges.
   - Visualize: Imagine yourself walking through a difficult situation with faith as your guide. How does this change your perspective and approach?

5. Daily Affirmation
   - Write: Create an affirmation centered on faith, such as "I trust in the divine plan for my life and walk in faith, knowing that I am guided and supported."
   - Repeat: Begin each day by reciting this affirmation, grounding yourself in faith as you navigate your journey.

6. Reflection on Progress
   - Monitor: At the end of each week, reflect on how your faith has influenced your actions and decisions. What changes have you noticed in your mindset and approach to challenges?
   - Adjust: If you find areas where faith has been difficult to apply, consider what might be holding you back and how you can deepen your trust.

Identity

- From Stone to Flesh (Ezekiel 36:26)
- The Power of a Simple Word (Psalm 119:105)
- Embracing Unity in the Face of Colorism and Racism (Galatians 3:28)

From Stone to Flesh

"I WILL GIVE YOU A NEW HEART AND PUT A NEW SPIRIT IN YOU; I WILL remove from you your heart of stone and give you a heart of flesh" (Ezekiel 36:26). Welcome to the backstage tour of my soul's sanctuary, where the cacophony of life's chaos meets the harmony of divine promises, shaping my identity in ways I never imagined. So grab your front-row seat and buckle up for the roller-coaster ride through the symphony of my life.

Now let's talk about Ezekiel 36:26—not your average Bible verse, mind you. It's more than just words on a page; it's a sacred contract, a transformative journey from a heart of stone to one of flesh. Think of it as getting a spiritual makeover, like going from a dull caterpillar to a vibrant butterfly.

But let's rewind a bit, shall we? Picture a young soul navigating the minefield of innocence, only to stumble into the dark shadows of deceit and violation. It's like trying to find your way through a maze blindfolded, with confusion and despair echoing off the walls.

In those darkest moments, I grappled with emotions heavier than a sack of potatoes—guilt, shame, and betrayal weighing me down like lead. It's as if life handed me a lemon the size of a watermelon and expected me to whip up a batch of lemonade.

And oh, the coping mechanisms! I buried those memories deeper than buried treasure, hoping they'd stay hidden forever. But as they say, time has a way of unraveling even the tightest knots, and before I knew it, the truth crashed down on me like a tidal wave, sweeping away my illusions faster than you can say, "Abracadabra."

But here's where the real magic kicked in. In the aftermath of revelation, I didn't just sit around twiddling my thumbs. Oh no! I grabbed life by the horns and wrestled those demons like a pro wrestler in the ring.

With newfound resilience and determination, I faced the shadows of my past head-on, like a knight taking on a fire-breathing dragon. And with each battle won, I emerged stronger, wearing my scars like badges of honor.

Through it all, the unwavering presence of a higher power guided me, offering solace in the darkest valleys and promising redemption. It was like having a GPS for the soul, leading me home through uncertainty.

Now, standing on the brink of a new dawn, I'm filled with purpose and hope. Though scars linger, they testify to my strength in adversity.

In the depths of molestation's darkness, I found not only pain but also hope—a beacon guiding me toward healing. If life's a concert, I'm ready to rock out with hope as my anthem and resilience as my dance partner.

Life Lesson

From this journey, I've learned that no darkness is insurmountable, and every scar tells a story of resilience. Through trials, we can find transformation, and amid chaos, there's harmony waiting to be discovered. So embrace the journey, for in every struggle lies the potential for growth and renewal.

The Power of a Simple Word

Psalm 119:105 shines with divine wisdom: "Your word is a lamp to my feet and a light to my path." Get ready for a wild ride through the pages of my life, from awkward pigtails to a semi-sophisticated young adult, where a simple lesson echoed in my ears like a catchy tune: "It doesn't hurt to speak, and it costs nothing to share a smile." Imagine it as if Hogwarts had a spell for making friends but with a sprinkle of everyday magic and a big dose of discovering and embracing identity.

In the tangled web of human interactions, I grappled with the idea that saying hi to someone who might respond with a poker face is like tiptoeing through a social minefield. It's the real-life version of trying to high-five a cat—you might get a friendly purr or end up with a claw in your hand.

But hold the phone, as the seeds of spiritual growth sprouted within me, the light bulb over my head flickered to life. Those simple gestures weren't just social formalities; they were like tossing pebbles into a pond, creating ripples of connection. A "hello" or a "good morning" wasn't merely a greeting; it was an invitation to brighten someone's day.

This section is my deep dive into the power of positivity as a superhero skill that can defy circumstances. God's goodness, intricately woven into our beings, becomes our compass, guiding us through the maze of life's choices. Drawing inspiration from the mysteries of life (no, not the ones you find in a detective novel), I embarked on a journey of self-discovery, figuring out how I dealt with life's curveballs.

The revelation hit me like a bolt of lightning—my life's trajectory was shaped by the deliberate choice to radiate positive vibes despite how others treated me. The intricate dance between faith and life's roller coaster became a testament to the transformative power of choosing positivity, righteousness, and all-around goodness. Despite the storms that threatened to turn my life into a bad-hair day, I clung to the unshakable belief that God's grace was paving the way forward.

This section isn't just a leisurely stroll down memory lane; it's a jubilant celebration of resilience born from the conscious decision to be a beacon of positivity. The journey from clueless innocence to semi-sophisticated maturity, marked by a simple yet profound lesson, showcases the world-changing impact that a kind word or a friendly smile can have on the intricate tapestry of human connection.

As we navigate the labyrinth of identity through existence, our words and smiles may be the beacons lighting up the path for ourselves and others. Let's foster connections that transcend the ordinary, embracing the extraordinary.

Life Lesson

Speak kind words and share smiles—like sprinkling glitter in a sometimes not-so-glamorous world.

Embracing Unity in the Face of Colorism and Racism

Galatians 3:28 lays the foundation for the epic saga of my life: *"There is neither Jew nor Gentile, neither slave nor free, nor is there male and female, for you are all one in Christ Jesus."* The journey through my identity was not always clear; it was often fraught with confusion, and in the beginning, I didn't have the language to name the forces acting upon me. I didn't fully understand the weight of colorism or racism, but I felt their presence—a quiet, persistent feeling that something was wrong with me.

Picture this: the canvas of my existence, vibrant with the colors of identity and belonging, yet tinged with uncertainty. Born to biracial parents, my skin tone was a constant but confusing protagonist in the unfolding drama of acceptance and otherness. It shaped how I was seen by others and, unknowingly, how I saw myself.

Let's rewind to the sun-soaked corridors of my predominantly Portuguese Catholic elementary school. It was a sanctuary where camaraderie enveloped me like a warm embrace, but even within that warmth, something unspoken stirred within me. I didn't know it then, but it was the subtle undercurrent of colorism. Envision a playground where fitting in and standing out danced in delicate balance, and although friendships blossomed, the feeling that I didn't quite belong lingered. At the time, I couldn't place why this feeling existed, but deep down, I sensed that I wasn't fully accepted for reasons beyond my control.

The real challenge, though, came not just in the playgrounds but within my own neighborhood. As I endeavored to forge deeper connections, I stumbled into the complex and often painful reality of colorism. Despite my best efforts to connect, my darker-skinned peers sometimes distanced themselves, labeling me a "white girl." I didn't understand why—why my skin seemed to separate us rather than bring us together. And in those moments of ostracization, I internalized the rejection, silently wondering if something was wrong with me, though I couldn't yet articulate the true cause of that hurt.

Fast forward to my undergraduate years: my parents, who had only completed primary education, deeply valued schooling, and instilled in me the belief that education was my key to success. Yet, as I entered higher education, the specter of racism emerged more clearly, though at first, it felt like the same uncomfortable sensation from my childhood—like something unseen was standing between me and the acceptance I sought. I vividly recall the painful moment when I was denied enrollment in a crucial class while watching a white peer glide effortlessly into the academic space. I remember thinking, *why doesn't this feel right? Is it me?*

The halls of academia, which should have been a sanctuary for learning, instead felt like a battlefield, though I couldn't immediately name the enemy. The injustice, the bias—it all felt wrong, but I had yet to fully grasp the deeper, systemic forces at play. I began to internalize the exclusion, wondering whether I simply didn't belong, all while a quiet voice inside urged me forward. This confusion transformed into the fuel that ignited my resolve to break through, to find answers, and to seek justice for myself and others who experienced the same silent barriers.

Amid this storm of doubt and confusion, I found my refuge in God. Though I couldn't always understand what was happening around me, I knew deep within that in His embrace, I was more than the labels imposed upon me. In those moments of doubt, my faith anchored me. Slowly, the feeling that something was wrong with me gave way to the understanding that what was truly wrong were the divisions and prejudices in the world around me. In God's eyes, I found clarity—a clarity that transcended the categories society tried to place upon me.

It's a narrative of discovering unity in Christ that reaches beyond the superficial judgments of the world. As I navigated the shadows of colorism and racism, my faith illuminated a path forward. The strength of my belief stripped the divisive labels of their power, and I began to understand that my value—and the value of every person—transcends the pigment of our skin. In this divine sanctuary, I discovered that I wasn't alone, and I certainly wasn't broken.

This journey taught me that while the world might seek to separate us by race or skin tone, we are united in our shared humanity and our belonging in Christ. In the eyes of God, we are not defined by the divisions of the world. We are one—one in love, one in purpose, and one in spirit.

Life Lesson

The diverse palette of humanity is meant to be celebrated, not divided. Let faith be the brush that paints a masterpiece of unity. Embracing our identities, rooted in love and faith, allows us to weave together the beautiful embroidery of human existence—each of us bound by the common thread of grace and understanding.

Identity Notes

Journey into the depths of your soul, where amid the cacophony of life's chaos, the divine promises of Ezekiel 36:26 stand as steadfast pillars of strength. Allow yourself to be guided by the radiant light of Psalm 119:105, illuminating the path forward with divine wisdom and clarity.

This exploration isn't merely a nostalgic trip down memory lane; it's a joyous celebration of resilience, rooted in a deliberate choice to radiate positivity amid life's ebbs and flows. From the innocence of youth to the wisdom of maturity, a powerful lesson emerges the transformative effect of kindness and connection on the fabric of our world.

Galatians 3:28 sets the stage for a profound journey of self-discovery as you grapple with the complexities of colorism and racism. Reflect deeply on how these issues have shaped your identity, and consider the multifaceted facets of your background, experiences, and values that contribute to the unique tapestry of who you are.

Amid life's tempests, envision yourself as a dancer on life's grand stage, gracefully navigating challenges, with resilience as your VIP pass. Embrace the storms as opportunities for growth and transformation, knowing that each trial shapes and molds you into the person you are meant to become.

Consider how your capacity to rebound from adversity shapes your understanding of self. Reflect on the moments of strength and courage that have carried you through the darkest of times, and recognize the inherent resilience that resides within you. As you delve deeper into the essence of your identity, may you emerge fortified with newfound understanding and resolve, ready to embrace the journey ahead with unwavering confidence and grace.

_____

_____

_____

_____

_____

_____

_____

_____

_____

_____

_____

_____

_____

Workbook Section

Deep Reflections

- Prompt: Reflecting on life's chaos and diversity, how do you define your identity? What facets of your background, experiences, and values contribute to shaping who you are? Amid life's tempests, do you envision yourself as a dancer, gracefully navigating challenges, with resilience as your VIP pass? How does your capacity to rebound from adversity shape your understanding of self?

Actionable Steps

1. Self-Exploration
   - Reflect: Write about the core elements that define your identity. Consider your cultural background, family traditions, personal experiences, and deeply held values.
   - Analyze: How do these aspects of your identity influence the way you view yourself and interact with the world around you?

2. Journaling Exercise
   - Explore: Describe a situation where you faced significant challenges or adversity. How did your identity help you navigate this period? Did it empower you, or were there aspects you needed to reconcile?
   - Contemplate: Think about a time when you had to adapt or change aspects of your identity. How did this experience affect your sense of self?

3. Visualizing Resilience
   - Envision: Picture yourself as a dancer moving through life's challenges. How does this imagery resonate with you? What qualities do you possess that allow you to move gracefully through adversity?

- Illustrate: Create a visual representation (a drawing, collage, or digital art) that symbolizes your identity and resilience. Reflect on how this process deepens your understanding of yourself.

4. Resilience in Action
   - Identify: Choose one area in your life where you currently face challenges. How can your understanding of your identity and resilience help you approach this situation differently?
   - Act: Implement a small but significant action that reflects your identity and demonstrates your resilience. This could be standing firm in your values, embracing a new challenge, or supporting someone else in their journey.

5. Daily Affirmation
   - Write: Craft an affirmation that reinforces your sense of identity and resilience, such as "I am grounded in my true self and navigate life's challenges with grace and strength."
   - Repeat: Recite this affirmation daily, letting it remind you of your inherent resilience and the power of your identity.

6. Reflection on Growth
   - Review: At the end of each week, reflect on how your understanding of your identity has evolved. How has your resilience been tested and strengthened?
   - Adjust: Consider any areas where you might need to further align your actions with your identity. What steps can you take to ensure that your identity continues to guide you through life's challenges?

Solitude

- In the Depths of Desolation (1 Corinthians 16:13–14)
- Seasons of the Heart (Jeremiah 29:11–13)
- God's Transformative Love (Psalm 143)

In the Depths of Desolation

"BE ON YOUR GUARD; STAND FIRM IN THE FAITH; BE COURAGEOUS; BE strong. Do everything in love" (1 Corinthians 16:13–14). Picture this section as a journey through the intricate shade of my life, a maze where the echoes of my thoughts reverberate against the walls of solitude. In the quiet corners of my existence, I sought solace, creating a clandestine sanctuary away from a world that seemed to shut its doors on love, especially within the intricate dance of my relationship with my mother—a connection entangled in malevolent forces.

Imagine diving into the recesses of my mind, discovering an uncharted space that transforms the struggles of reality into the serene shores of a beautiful, metaphorical beach. It's like an escape from the storms outside, a place where the whispers of biblical verses, ingrained in me by my Catholic upbringing, become a distant yet soothing melody. "Ask and it shall be given, seek and you shall find, knock and the door will open." Fueled by these words, I yearned for answers in the silence of my secluded haven, hoping that God would unveil the mysteries that shrouded my reality. But, alas, as my pleas echoed in the caverns of my mind, the response from the divine seemed to play hide-and-seek, leaving me grappling with feelings of abandonment.

Prepare to hear about paradox. In the depths of desolation, the teachings that once anchored my spirit now echoed in the emptiness around me. "Be watchful, stand firm in the faith, act like men, be strong. Let all that you do be done in love." These words became my mantra, a resilient call to stand firm when faced with solitude, to embody strength in the face of God's apparent silence. It's like being handed a survival guide in the wilderness of the mind.

As I contemplated the meaning behind the divine serenity, my beliefs trembled. Was it a test of my strength, an invitation to forge a more profound connection, or a glimpse into a divine plan beyond my comprehension? In the depths of desolation, I found myself navigating uncharted waters of faith, clinging to the hope that love would eventually illuminate the shadows, guiding me through the profound silence that enveloped my world.

Life Lesson

Embrace the paradoxes, navigate the uncharted waters, and find strength in the echoes of your resilience. The profound silence may be the backdrop to a divine symphony waiting to unfold.

Seasons of the Heart

"'For I know the plans I have for you,' declares the Lord, 'plans to prosper you and not to harm you, plans to give you hope and a future. Then you will call on me and come and pray to me, and I will listen to you. You will seek me and find me when you seek me with all your heart'" (Jeremiah 29:11–13). Welcome to the whimsical embroidery of my life—a poetic journey through the seasons of the heart. Picture this: relationships are like a high-wire act in a circus, balancing on the delicate tightrope of emotions while juggling the unpredictability of life's circus monkeys. As I tiptoed through the tightrope, I found myself gracefully transitioning through summers of joy, autumns of reflection, winters of challenge, and springs of renewal. But oh, amid this heart-fluttering choreography, finding solitude became my elusive unicorn, my holy grail.

In the mystical realm of Jeremiah 29:11–13, divine assurance echoes like a celestial choir: "For I know the plans I have for you ... plans to give you hope and a future." It was as if the heavens opened up, and I embarked on a fantastical journey—a treasure hunt through the enchanted forest of God's

Word. Here, amid the twinkling fireflies and whispering trees, solitude transformed me like a caterpillar emerging from its cocoon, revealing the vibrant wings of self-love and inherent worthiness.

Join me in navigating the treacherous waters of love and friendship—a journey that felt like paddling a canoe through a tempestuous sea of emotions. Seeking a partner who shared my devotion to God was like searching for a needle in a haystack—only the haystack was made of sacred scriptures, and the needle was a soulmate. I was Indiana Jones, armed with faith as my whip and God's grace as my fedora, on a divine scavenger hunt through the jungle of love.

But ah, identifying a good partner was like trying to find Waldo in a sea of stripes. It required patience, perseverance, and a keen eye for red flags. Yet amid the occasional missteps and comedic pratfalls, there was a hidden treasure: solitude within the rhythm—a quiet moment amid the cacophony of life's orchestra.

And oh, the mourning of relationships—like a dirge played on a loop by a sorrowful mariachi band. Have you ever tried to sing along to a sad song while wearing a sombrero? It's a sight to behold. Letting go felt like saying goodbye to a beloved pet rock—oddly painful yet oddly necessary for growth. Reflecting on the journey, I realized that even heartaches had a solo in life's symphony—a poignant melody that added depth to the composition.

Life Lesson

So what's the lesson in this madcap adventure of love and solitude? Love like it's the summer, reflect like it is autumn, face challenges like winter, and renew like spring. And amid the grand dance of relationships, remember consistency is our choreography, and God is our partner. So let's grab our dancing shoes and tango through the seasons together, shall we?

God's Transformative Love

"Let the morning bring me word of your unfailing love, for I have put my trust in you. Show me the way I should go, for to you I entrust my life" (Psalm 143:8). Welcome to the thrilling saga of my life—a tale that could rival the drama of a Shakespearean play. Picture this: the poetic verses of Psalm 143 serve as a spotlight, illuminating the profound truth that God's unwavering love holds the power to transform us, offering solace amid life's tumultuous journey. And oh, buckle up, because I'm about to spill the beans on how I found solitude, even amid the heartaches.

Imagine me ensnared in the labyrinth of an abusive relationship. It wasn't just your run-of-the-mill breakup; it was a tangled mess worthy of a blockbuster movie plot. The emotional bonds felt stronger than industrial-grade superglue, and trying to untangle them was like attempting a magic trick without a manual. So I did what any sensible person would do—I called in the avengers of the spiritual realm and sought solace from God, praying for strength to navigate this twisted maze.

And guess what? God delivered with a plot twist that could rival any Hollywood blockbuster. He unveiled a dark chapter from my father's past, which you'll find more juicy details about in the "Two-Timing Tomfoolery" section. It was as if God said, "Hold on. There's more to this story." Ironically, this revelation became my ticket to freedom. It was like being handed a secret map to escape the labyrinth, and with newfound courage, I turned the page on that toxic chapter and embraced a fresh start.

Through this tumultuous journey, I stumbled upon a profound truth: nobody's perfect. It's like we're all characters in a cosmic comedy, each trying to find our groove on the dance floor of life. And let me tell you, discerning how much imperfection one can tolerate is like trying to pick the right dance partner in a crowded ballroom.

Believing in God's unconditional love is nothing short of transformative. It's like discovering you have a VIP pass to the greatest show on earth. It inspires us to live mindfully, knowing that we're under the loving gaze of our Creator. Picture God sitting in the audience with a bag of popcorn, cheering you on as you navigate life's twists and turns.

In this chapter of my journey, I've unearthed the transformative power of God's love—a force that empowers, redeems, and guides us. It's like undergoing a divine makeover, where solitude becomes the cocoon that transforms us into beautiful butterflies.

Life Lesson

Embrace imperfection, dance through life's challenges with divine love as your partner, and always be prepared for those unexpected plot twists. After all, every twist and turn is just another opportunity for divine transformation.

Solitude Notes

Embark on a profound journey guided by the timeless wisdom of 1 Corinthians 16:13–14, where life's paradoxes are embraced, uncharted waters are navigated, and strength is drawn from the depths of resilience. In the profound silence that envelops us, recognize it as the backdrop to a divine symphony awaiting its grand unfoldment.

Allow Jeremiah 29:11–13 to serve as your compass through the whirlwind adventure of love and solitude. Here, you are urged to love passionately, reflect introspectively, face challenges with fortitude, and renew your spirit like the blossoming spring. Amid the grand dance of relationships, find solace in the consistency of your choreography, with God as your steadfast partner.

Embrace the wisdom of Psalm 143, encouraging you to embrace imperfection, glide through life's trials with divine love, and remain prepared for the unexpected twists that each day may bring. For within these twists lie opportunities for divine transformation and growth.

Together, these passages illuminate the path to finding solace in solitude, navigating life's seasons with grace, and embracing the transformative power of divine love. Allow yourself to be enveloped by the whispers of the divine, finding peace and serenity amid the chaos of the world.

_____

_____

_____

_____

_____

_____

_____

_____

_____

_____

_____

_____

_____

_____

_____

Workbook Section

Deep Reflections

- Prompt: Amidst life's grand tapestry, where do you find solace in solitude? Reflecting on the echoes of resilience within profound silence, do you see it as the backdrop to a divine symphony waiting to unfold? As you journey through the seasons of love, reflection, challenges, and renewal, how do you navigate the dance of relationships with consistency as your choreography and God as your partner? Moreover, in embracing imperfection and navigating unexpected plot twists, how does divine love guide you through the labyrinth of life's challenges?

Actionable Steps

1. Embracing Solitude
   - Reflect: Spend time in solitude and reflect on where you find peace in being alone. How does solitude allow you to connect with your inner self and divine guidance?
   - Write: Describe moments when solitude has provided clarity or comfort in your life. How does it serve as a foundation for your resilience?

2. Journaling Exercise
   - Explore: Write about a time when silence and solitude played a crucial role in your spiritual or personal growth. How did these moments shape your understanding of yourself and your relationship with God?
   - Contemplate: Consider the role of solitude in your daily life. How can you intentionally create space for it, allowing it to become a regular practice?

3. Divine Symphony Visualization
    -   Envision: Imagine the silence of solitude as the backdrop to a divine symphony. What melodies or harmonies do you hear when you quiet your mind and listen deeply?
    -   Illustrate: Create a piece of art or a written reflection that symbolizes this divine symphony. How does this visualization deepen your connection to divine love and guidance?

4. Navigating Relationships
    -   Identify: Reflect on your relationships and how you navigate them with consistency and faith. How does your relationship with God influence the way you engage with others?
    -   Act: Choose one relationship where you can apply more intentionality, using solitude to reflect on how you can show up more consistently and lovingly.

5. Embracing Imperfection
    -   Accept: Acknowledge the imperfections in your life and relationships. How does embracing these imperfections allow you to grow and learn?
    -   Act: Identify one area where you can let go of perfectionism and allow divine love to guide you through unexpected challenges. What small steps can you take to trust in this guidance?

6. Daily Affirmation
    -   Write: Create an affirmation centered on solitude, divine love, and resilience, such as "In the silence of solitude, I find divine love guiding me through every challenge with grace and strength."
    -   Repeat: Begin each day with this affirmation, grounding yourself in the peace that solitude and divine guidance provide.

7. Reflection on Journey

- Monitor: At the end of each week, reflect on how solitude has influenced your spiritual journey and relationships. What insights have you gained from embracing quiet moments and divine guidance?

- Adjust: Consider any areas where you might need to deepen your practice of solitude or trust in divine love. What steps can you take to continue navigating life's challenges with resilience and faith?

Transformation

- The Transformative Mirror (Romans 12:2)
- A First Lady's Journey through Church Circles and Self-Discovery (1 Timothy 3:1–7)
- Harmony in the Therapeutic Symphony (Isaiah 55:11)

The Transformative Mirror

"DO NOT CONFORM TO THE PATTERN OF THIS WORLD, BUT BE transformed by the renewing of your mind. Then you will be able to test and approve what God's will is—his good, pleasing, and perfect will" (Romans 12:2). Picture this: it's a regular day, and I'm doing the usual—admiring myself in the mirror, diligently replicating what society deems beautiful. The allure of fashion, grooming, and physical presentation shrouded my perception like a spell. Who hasn't fallen for judging and seeking validation based on outward appearances? We're all human, right?

But then, cue the fateful day when God decided to play director and orchestrate a revelation that shattered my carefully constructed facade. It wasn't just about the physical features staring back at me; it was like the cosmic curtain lifting to reveal a more profound, unseen ugliness. Imagine thinking you're tuning into a rom-com and ending up in a psychological thriller. That was my mirror moment.

This wasn't a cue for a dramatic breakdown but rather the spotlight for a transformative journey. I turned to God, not wishing for the perfect Instagram-able appearance but with a fervent prayer for an inner beauty that would radiate through every facet of my being—thoughts, words, and actions included. It was a plea for beauty that transcends the surface, something unattainable through the magic wand of cosmetics.

But let's be honest; prayers alone don't cut it. This journey demanded more than just a spiritual awakening; it called for a holistic transformation. I embraced lifestyle changes, committed myself to continuous self-improvement, and understood that genuine beauty isn't confined to the external. It's like trying to decode the secret recipe of inner beauty.

As the sections of my transformative journey unfolded, the plot thickened. I stumbled upon a profound realization—true beauty is more than just fleeting visual appeal. The external features might catch your eye, but the attitude and character define a beauty that lasts longer than the latest beauty trend. It's like realizing the book is way better than the movie adaptation.

I witnessed firsthand that individuals, despite their outward charm, could be marred by the impact of hurtful words and actions. This lesson is etched in my soul, emphasizing the paramount importance of cultivating an inner beauty that radiates far beyond the confines of the physical mirror. It's like getting a backstage pass to the show, where the character development steals the spotlight.

Life Lesson

True beauty isn't skin deep; it's character deep. The mirror might reflect your appearance, but the accurate reflection happens through your attitudes, kindness, and the transformative light of God's grace radiating from within. So in the grand play of life, remember—you're the lead character, and your inner beauty steals the show. Cue the standing ovation.

A First Lady's Journey through Church Circles and Self-Discovery

"Here is a trustworthy saying: Whoever aspires to be an overseer desires a noble task. Now the overseer is to be above reproach, faithful to his wife, temperate, self-controlled, respectable, hospitable, able to teach, not given to drunkenness, not violent but gentle, not quarrelsome, not a lover of money. He must manage his own family well and see that his children obey him, and he must do so in a manner worthy of full respect. (If anyone does not know how to manage his own family, how can he take care of God's church?) He must not be a recent convert, or he may become conceited and fall under the same judgment as the devil. He must also have a good reputation with outsiders so that he will not fall into disgrace and into the devil's trap" (1 Timothy 3:1–7). Life in the church can be quite the transformational journey, especially when you're thrust into the spotlight as the esteemed "first lady." Now, let me tell you, being a first lady ain't all fancy hats and Sunday brunches. Oh no, it's like being the CEO of a company you never applied to work for!

From my early days in the Catholic pews to hopping around different denominations like a spiritual nomad—Christ Church, Pentecostal, you name it—I've seen it all. And let me tell you, navigating those church circles can sometimes feel like tiptoeing through a minefield in stilettos.

Picture this: me, trying to spread love and light in a traditional Baptist church, only to feel like an alien crash-landing at a square dance. The members eyed me like I was a slice of pineapple on a pizza—completely out of place. Despite my efforts to dive headfirst into youth and women ministries, I was met with more side-eye than a catwalk model at a dog show.

And oh, the gossip! It flowed through those pews like holy water at a baptism. I could practically hear the whispers echoing off the stained glass windows. It was like high school all over again, except this time the drama was blessed by the pastor.

But wait, it gets better. Just when I thought I'd seen it all, my dear husband—bless his heart—decided to throw a curveball by indulging in a little extracurricular activity with a parishioner. Well, that was the straw that broke the camel's back, or in this case, the pew that broke the pastor's spouse.

But you know what they say, every cloud has a silver lining. And in my case, that silver lining was divorce. Yes, you heard me right—divorce! Liberating doesn't even begin to describe the feeling of shedding the title of "first lady" and reclaiming my identity. No more lonely nights at church functions, pretending to enjoy small talk with Sister So-and-So's fifth cousin twice removed.

Through it all, I've learned that transformation often comes disguised as chaos. Sometimes you have to wade through the murky waters of judgment and betrayal to find the shore of self-discovery. And let me tell you, darling, once you reach that shore, there's no turning back—only forward, into the radiant sunrise of your empowerment.

Life Lesson

In the turbulence of church politics and personal trials, I unearthed a profound truth: authenticity is the cornerstone of empowerment. No amount of societal titles or expectations can mask the beauty of embracing one's true self. The journey through the wilderness of judgment and betrayal unveiled a resilient spirit within me, one that thrived on the shores of self-discovery.

Through the storm, I learned that true transformation isn't about conforming to the expectations of others but about embracing the authenticity of one's journey. It's about recognizing that adversity, though daunting, is often the catalyst for growth. And it's about understanding that the greatest empowerment lies not in the titles we hold but in the strength of character and integrity with which we navigate life's twists and turns.

So, to all those navigating their own tumultuous seas, I offer this beacon of hope: stay true to yourself, for it is in the authenticity of your journey that you will find the strength to weather any storm and emerge victorious on the shores of self-discovery.

Harmony in the Therapeutic Symphony

Once upon a time, in the chaotic symphony of life, I stumbled upon a refuge, an oasis for my weary soul—a therapist's office. Isaiah 55:11 whispered in the background, "My word that goes out from my mouth: It will not return to me empty but will accomplish what I desire and achieve the purpose for which I sent it." Little did I know that those words would become the guiding melody of my therapy journey.

Picture this: a cozy room with soft hues, plush chairs that seemed to envelop you in a warm embrace, and a gentle aroma of soothing lavender lingering in the air. The atmosphere alone was a balm for my worn-out spirit. It was like entering a sanctuary where judgment dared not tread.

As I settled into the snug embrace of the therapeutic cocoon, I realized the power of having someone trustworthy to confide in. It was not merely a dialogue but a dance of words, a waltz of vulnerability, and a safe space to unravel the tapestry of my innermost thoughts and experiences. My therapist was not a devourer of secrets but a guardian of the sacred, offering a haven where I could lay bare my soul without fear.

Therapy was my compass through the labyrinth of life's complexities. My trusted confidant didn't just nod empathetically but, armed with wisdom and kindness, provided sensible solutions to the tumultuous storms I faced. It was like having a wise wizard in my corner, casting spells of clarity and perspective on the foggy landscape of my mind.

Permit me to inject a touch of humor into this tale of transformation. Imagine my inner struggles as a theatrical play, complete with exaggerated sighs and eye rolls. Therapy was my backstage pass, allowing me to step out of the theatrical chaos and view my life as a comedy of errors rather than a tragic opera. Laughter is a potent elixir for the soul.

In this roller coaster of self-discovery, I stumbled upon a therapist who was a guide and a coconspirator in the grand heist of becoming the best version of myself. It was not just about talking but unraveling the layers, peeling off the masks, and discovering the unfiltered authenticity beneath.

My therapist, a beacon of strength, empowered me to confront my challenges head-on. Like a personal trainer for the mind, pushing me gently but firmly, helping me flex the muscles of resilience and courage. With each session, I emerged a little more unburdened, a tad more enlightened, and much stronger.

As I reflect on this journey, I'm flooded with gratitude for the serendipity that led me to a therapist who didn't just understand but resonated with the symphony of my struggles. It's like finding the perfect dance partner—every step, every twirl, a harmonious sync of understanding and support.

Lesson Learned

And now, dear reader, the curtains draw to a close with a life lesson forged in the crucible of my therapeutic voyage. Isaiah 55:11 reminds us that words, once spoken, can shape destinies. Similarly, the words we share with ourselves and others can build bridges or erect barriers.

So here's the lesson—embrace the power of your spoken and unspoken words. Be mindful of the narratives you weave and surround yourself with those who nurture your growth. Like a well-crafted symphony, let your life unfold with purpose, guided by the echoes of your inner truths and the wisdom gained through the dance of words and understanding. After all, in the grand theater of life, we are not merely spectators but active participants, shaping our stories one word at a time.

Transformation Notes

Enter the realm of profound transformation guided by the illuminating truths of Romans 12:2, where the essence of true beauty transcends surface appearances, radiating from the depths of our character and the transformative light of God's grace within. As we take our place upon life's grand stage, let us remember that our inner beauty shines brightest, deserving of recognition akin to a standing ovation.

Crafted with the intent to evoke personal reflection, these reflections beckon you to delve into your own journey of faith and self-discovery. Drawing inspiration from 1 Timothy 3:1–7, the passage resonates with your experiences amid the turbulence of life's challenges and spiritual growth. It illuminates the profound truth that authenticity serves as the cornerstone of your empowerment, urging you to reflect on how you navigate your wilderness of trials and judgments.

Through this introspection, you recognize the transformative power of staying true to yourself amid societal pressures. It extends a message of hope, reminding you to find strength in your authenticity and encouraging you to trust that your unique journey holds the keys to weathering any storm and emerging victorious on the path to self-discovery.

Find inspiration in the guiding wisdom of Isaiah 55:11, which urges us to wield the power of our words with mindfulness, recognizing them as the architects of our reality. Let us craft narratives that reflect our inner truths and surround ourselves with individuals who nurture our growth and inspire us to reach new heights.

Envision your life as a symphony unfolding with purposeful harmony, guided by the echoes of your deepest convictions and the wisdom gained through your experiences. In this grand theater of existence, we are not mere spectators but active participants, shaping our stories with intention, one word at a time.

Embrace the transformative journey that lies ahead, knowing that each step you take and each word you speak has the power to shape your reality and lead you closer to the fullness of your divine purpose. May you emerge from this journey fortified with newfound understanding and resolve, ready to embrace the transformative power of God's grace and the limitless potential within yourself.

_____

_____

_____

_____

_____

_____

_____

_____

Workbook Section

Deep Reflections

- Prompt: Reflecting on the profound lesson of inner beauty and the transformative power of words, how do you perceive your role as the lead character in the grand play of life? How do you actively cultivate authenticity in your journey of faith and self-discovery amid life's challenges and societal pressures? As you navigate the narratives you weave and the relationships you cultivate, how do you harness the wisdom gained through the dance of words and understanding to shape your story with purpose? Moreover, how do you allow the echoes of your inner truths and the guiding light of grace to orchestrate your transformation journey in the symphony of existence?

Actionable Steps

1. Embracing Inner Beauty
    - Reflect: Spend time contemplating what inner beauty means to you. How do your actions, thoughts, and words reflect this inner beauty? How does it shape your interactions with others?
    - Write: Describe moments in your life when you felt truly beautiful from the inside out. How did these moments influence your journey of self-discovery and faith?

2. Journaling Exercise
    - Explore: Reflect on your role as the lead character in your life. How have you embraced this role, and in what ways do you sometimes shy away from it? What steps can you take to fully embody this role with authenticity?
    - Contemplate: Write about the narratives you've created in your life. How do these narratives align with your true self and your journey of transformation?

3. Cultivating Authenticity
    -   Identify: Think about areas in your life where you feel pressure to conform to societal expectations. How can you practice authenticity in these areas, staying true to your values and beliefs?
    -   Act: Choose one situation this week where you will consciously practice authenticity, even if it feels challenging. Reflect on the outcome and how it affects your sense of self.

4. Harnessing Wisdom
    -   Envision: Picture the words and wisdom you've gained throughout your life as a dance that shapes your narrative. How can you use this wisdom to guide your decisions and interactions?
    -   Illustrate: Create a visual or written representation of how the transformative power of words has shaped your life. How does this representation inspire you to continue growing and evolving?

5. Guided Meditation
    -   Focus: Spend time in meditation, allowing the echoes of your inner truths and the light of grace to guide your thoughts. How do these elements support your transformation journey?
    -   Visualize: Imagine your life as a symphony, with each experience adding to the harmony of your existence. How does this imagery help you embrace your journey with grace and purpose?

6. Daily Affirmation
    -   Write: Create an affirmation that reflects your commitment to authenticity, inner beauty, and transformation, such as "I embrace my journey with authenticity and grace, allowing the wisdom of my inner truths to guide me."
    -   Repeat: Start each day by reciting this affirmation, grounding yourself in the transformative power of your words and actions.

7. Reflection on Progress
   - Monitor: At the end of each week, reflect on how you've embraced your role as the lead character in your life's story. How has your understanding of inner beauty and authenticity evolved?
   - Adjust: Consider any areas where you may need to further align your actions with your inner truths. What steps can you take to continue your journey of transformation with purpose and grace?

Purpose

- Illuminating the Darkness with God's Beauty (Romans 8:28)
- Rediscovering the Lost Pieces Within (Proverbs 16:3)
- Storms as Stepping Stones (James 1:12–14)

Illuminating the Darkness with God's Beauty

"AND WE KNOW THAT IN ALL THINGS GOD WORKS FOR THE GOOD OF those who love him, who have been called according to his purpose" (Romans 8:28). Step into the rhythm where the text sets the stage, whispering secrets like a wise mentor in a shadowy corner. Here, I invite you to the recesses of my soul, where shadows of severe depression once painted my existence in hues of worthlessness and profound sadness. Each day felt like navigating an abyss, where even the simplest tasks morphed into monumental challenges, leaving me questioning my purpose. But hold on, the story takes a turn.

Cue the tears and the daily ritual of crying. Picture it: I am attempting to tackle life's hurdles, but each step feels like wading through quicksand. The haunting question echoes in my mind: *What is wrong with me?* and *Do I even have a purpose?* It's a tough spot. But amid the tumult, I discovered a lifeline—the transformative power of prayer.

Let me tell you, prayer became my compass, guiding me through the haze of despair. In those moments when darkness threatened to engulf me, prayer was the force that gradually lifted me from the depths. It wasn't just a Band-Aid; it was the key to unlocking healing.

Allow yourself to imagine a beautiful sanctuary amid nature's wonders. There, I'd pour my heart into God, thanking Him for His boundless goodness and guidance. It wasn't just about reciting words but finding solace amid creation. This section reveals a profound truth—praising God isn't just a duty; it's a pathway to embracing His beauty to find purpose.

But let's add some flair to this narrative. Picture me stepping outside, breathing in the fragrance of flowers, gazing at the azure sky, and having a moment with the resident symphony of birds and animals. This was some of what I was able to experience during a church retreat to help manage my depression. It's like a divine rendezvous with nature, all while marveling at the intricate beauty of family and children. It's not just about saying, "Thank You, God." It's about looking around and exclaiming, "Wow, look at what God has and continues to do!"

In the storm of depression, praising God became my beacon of hope. This section is an ode to the transformative power of gratitude—a reminder that, even in the darkest moments, embracing God's beauty can light the path to healing and restoration. It's a testament that, with faith and gratitude, one can find light within the shadows and emerge more robust, resilient, and deeply attuned to the beauty surrounding us.

Life Lesson

When the shadows loom large, step outside, take a deep breath, and let the symphony of life remind you that God's beauty is ever present, and there is a purpose for us. Embrace it, celebrate it, and allow it to guide you through life's storms.

Rediscovering the Lost Pieces Within

Guided by the timeless wisdom of Proverbs 16:3, "Commit to the Lord whatever you do, and he will establish your plans," I invite you into the labyrinth of love, where my journey becomes a poignant narrative. Picture it: a quest to become someone's everything—lover, wife, mother, and all the extras. Little did I know, this quest led me down a rabbit hole where the lines between self and significant other blurred into a hazy illusion. It became my quest to find what my purpose was after losing myself to becoming someone else's everything.

Let's inject a bit of humor into this. Imagine me juggling roles like a circus performer, attempting to be the panacea for someone's struggles.

Spoiler alert: it didn't end well. Instead, I found myself in a shadowy realm of mental and physical abuse, oppression, and the gradual erosion of my sense of self. It's like signing up for a thrilling adventure but ending up in a twisted plotline.

As I sacrificed my interests and friendships, I danced to a solitary rhythm, forgetting the sweet sound of laughter with friends and losing touch with who I was and what my purpose in life was. It was like entering a sci-fi movie where the boundaries between self-care and self-sacrifice vanished, leaving me as a silhouette unrecognizable even to myself.

And then the revelation struck. Drumroll, please! I had lost myself in the pursuit of saving another. This section isn't a sob story; it's a testament to the resilience of the human spirit and the graceful guidance of God. It's a narrative of purposeful rediscovery, a phoenix rising from the ashes of misplaced love.

Picture a blockbuster movie where the hero embarks on a quest for self-love and purpose, armed with the wisdom gained from a tumultuous journey. In the crucible of intense love, I discovered a profound truth: true love, aligned with God's plan, doesn't demand sacrificing your identity and purpose. Instead, it invites you to love yourself as God loves you—unconditionally and wholly.

Allow me to add a touch of romance to this section. It's a journey of emerging from the shadows, a quest for self-love that's more epic than a Hollywood romance. In losing myself to God, I found the strength to rediscover and rebuild my identity. The echoes of Proverbs were my compass—delighting in the Lord became the North Star guiding me to the desires of my heart, desires aligned with the profound love and purpose woven into the fabric of my existence.

So, dear reader, let this section inspire you. May it inspire you to embark on your quest, rediscover your lost pieces, and recognize that your most authentic identity thrives and blooms in God's love and your purpose.

Life Lesson

Love yourself a little more each day. God does, and it's a love that transforms.

Storms as Stepping Stones

Welcome to my life's chronicles—a tale illuminated by the timeless wisdom spoken of James 1:12–14, "Blessed is the one who perseveres under trial because, having stood the test, that person will receive the crown of life that the Lord has promised to those who love him. When tempted, no one should say, 'God is tempting me.' For God cannot be tempted by evil, nor does he tempt anyone, but each person is tempted when they are dragged away by their own evil desire and enticed." This isn't just any story; it's a saga where stumbling blocks are transformed into stepping stones and God's enduring goodness shines through the stormy clouds. It's a narrative where purpose arises from the depths of abuse, turning anguish into triumph.

Picture this: the revelation of my family's secret of physical abuse between my parents became both a burden and a catalyst for transformation. I can still vividly recall those harrowing moments when I witnessed my dad's drunken fury, his actions like thunderclaps echoing through our home. It was a plot twist that led to a breathtaking climax—one where God's guiding light pierced through the darkest shadows of my life.

Leaving behind my toxic relationship felt like navigating treacherous waters, all while vowing to break the cycle of abuse inherited from my parents. If life were a movie, this would be the scene where the hero faces their greatest challenge. Amid the crashing waves of uncertainty, God's light became my steadfast lighthouse, guiding me through the tempest. It wasn't just about survival; it was a divine invitation to learn, grow, and emerge stronger.

As I began the arduous task of rebuilding my life after the storm, I discovered that God's purpose wasn't to leave us broken but to empower us to become resilient warriors. This section isn't about dwelling on victimhood;

it's a triumphant march over adversity. It's a journey that beckons us to embrace storms as opportunities for growth and enlightenment.

Think of each trial as a metamorphic experience—a divine reshaping of our souls. It's as if God whispers, "Hey, I know it's tough, but trust Me, you'll emerge from this stronger and wiser." Life's storms aren't roadblocks; they're invitations for positive change. They have the power to turn pain into a catalyst for our purposeful transformation.

Life Lesson

So here's the life lesson: in the crucible of physical and verbal abuse, God shapes us into resilient beings capable of weathering any storm. It's not about avoiding difficulties but about navigating through them with unwavering purpose. This section is an invitation to view stumbling blocks not as obstacles but as stepping stones leading to a triumphant future—a future bathed in the radiant light that awaits beyond the clouds. May it inspire others to dance through their storms, knowing that on the other side, they'll find stepping stones to a brighter, more triumphant future.

Purpose Notes

Embark on a profound journey of self-discovery guided by deep spiritual insights as we seek meaning and resilience amid the trials of life. Romans 8:28 serves as a beacon of hope, reminding us of the enduring presence of God's beauty, offering comfort even in the darkest moments, and guiding us through life's tumultuous storms.

Let Proverbs 16:3 be our guiding light as we embark on this journey of self-discovery, acknowledging that our true identity flourishes within the embrace of God's love and purpose. As we nurture self-love, we are uplifted and transformed by the boundless love of our Creator.

Embrace the wisdom of James 1:12–14, viewing adversity as an opportunity for growth that molds us into resilient individuals capable of overcoming life's greatest challenges. Each obstacle we face becomes a stepping stone toward a triumphant future, where the radiant light of God's love awaits beyond the clouds.

This section extends an invitation to embrace life's obstacles with courage and resilience, knowing that on the other side lies a path to a brighter and more fulfilling destiny. May it inspire others to navigate their storms with grace and faith, trusting in the transformative power of God's love to lead them toward a future filled with hope and purpose.

_____
_____
_____
_____
_____
_____
_____
_____
_____
_____
_____
_____
_____
_____

Workbook Section

Deep Reflections

- Prompt: Reflecting on the lessons learned amid life's storms and shadows, how do you perceive your journey toward discovering purpose? As you navigate challenges and embrace the transformative love surrounding you, how do you view stumbling blocks—as obstacles or stepping stones toward a brighter future? Moreover, how does unwavering faith guide you through the crucible of difficulties, shaping you into a resilient being capable of weathering any storm? In contemplating these lessons, how do you envision your path forward, illuminated by the radiant light that awaits beyond the clouds and driven by the purpose that arises from overcoming adversity?

Actionable Steps

1. Understanding Purpose
   - Reflect: Think about significant challenges you have faced and the lessons you have learned from them. How have these experiences shaped your understanding of your life's purpose?
   - Write: Describe a moment when you discovered a new aspect of your purpose through adversity. How did this revelation affect your journey and outlook?

2. Journaling Exercise
   - Explore: Write about a recent stumbling block or difficulty you faced. How did you perceive it—as an obstacle or a stepping stone? What did you learn from this experience?
   - Contemplate: Reflect on how you can shift your perspective on challenges to view them as opportunities for growth. How can this change in perspective help you move forward?

3. Navigating Challenges
   - Identify: Identify a current challenge or difficulty you are facing. How can you use your unwavering faith to guide you through this situation?
   - Act: Develop a plan for how you will approach this challenge with faith and resilience. What steps can you take to stay grounded and focused on your purpose?

4. Harnessing Transformative Love
   - Envision: Visualize the transformative love surrounding you as a guiding force in your journey. How does this love help you navigate through the storms and shadows of life?
   - Illustrate: Create a visual representation or a written reflection that captures the essence of this transformative love and its role in your journey toward purpose.

5. Path Forward
   - Reflect: Consider how your path forward is illuminated by the lessons learned and the light that awaits beyond your current challenges. How does this vision shape your goals and actions?
   - Plan: Outline a plan for how you will move forward, driven by the purpose that arises from overcoming adversity. What specific actions will you take to align with this purpose?

6. Daily Affirmation
   - Write: Craft an affirmation that encapsulates your commitment to discovering and living out your purpose, such as "I embrace life's challenges as opportunities for growth, guided by unwavering faith and illuminated by the light of purpose."
   - Repeat: Recite this affirmation daily to reinforce your focus on purpose and resilience.

7. Reflection on Progress
    - Monitor: At the end of each week, review how your perspective on purpose and challenges has evolved. How has your faith guided you through difficulties?
    - Adjust: Consider any adjustments you need to make in your approach to challenges or in your pursuit of purpose. What steps can you take to continue moving forward with clarity and conviction?

Freedom

- A Journey from Stifled to Empowered (Colossians 3:21)
- Blossom of Resilience (Ezekiel 7:10)
- Unveiling the Miracles (1 John 4:8)

A Journey from Stifled to Empowered

"FATHERS, DO NOT PROVOKE YOUR CHILDREN, LEST THEY BECOME discouraged" (Colossians 3:21). Welcome to the vivid tapestry of my childhood—a canvas painted with the stifling strokes of "children should be seen and not heard," a mantra that echoed through the corridors of my existence like a nagging alarm clock—silence draped over me like a heavy quilt, smothering my budding sense of freedom.

But rebellion simmered within me like a pot left unattended on the stove, just waiting to boil over. One fateful day, I decided to flip the script, to break free from the confining chains of this stifling mantra. Little did I know that my innocent quest for self-expression would be interpreted by my mother as an act of outright rebellion and disrespect. Living under her watchful eye became a delicate dance, where her well-meaning intentions clashed with my burning desire for autonomy. It was like trying to square dance with a grizzly bear—awkward, confusing, and downright dangerous.

And let's not forget the extracurricular extravaganza—a whirlwind of activities meticulously chosen for me, from ballet to guitar lessons, with a sprinkle of usher duties at church thrown in for good measure. Each activity had its merits, sure, but the absence of my voice in these decisions felt like being handed a plate of spaghetti without a fork. I longed for the freedom to choose my path, to explore interests beyond the realm of musical instruments and usher badges.

Picture a young me navigating adult situations like a lost puppy stumbling through a minefield—an unexpected glimpse into my parents' love lives and peculiar visits to the gun club with my father, where the clink of glasses harmonized with the chorus of gambling and smoke. These experiences, though beyond my years, left indelible marks, serving as cautionary tales of the importance of shielding children from certain aspects of adult life.

But amid the chaos, God's guidance emerged as a guiding beacon, gradually lifting the heavy cloak of imposed silence. Finding my voice wasn't an overnight revelation; it was a journey of patient growth and divine intervention, like trying to teach a parrot to sing opera.

Currently a parent myself, I wholeheartedly advocate for a new mantra: children should be seen and heard! It's my mission to shatter the cycle of silence, ensuring that my children never feel stifled in their pursuit of self-expression. Having embarked on my quest for freedom, I am determined not to confine others with unnecessary constraints. Thus, I instill in my children the value of respectful self-expression, empowering them to raise their voices without fear of being silenced.

This transformative odyssey isn't just a chapter in my life story; it's an ongoing saga of growth and resilience, a testament to the enduring spirit of humanity. Each day unfolds a new chapter in the journey from silence to empowerment, proving that even the most oppressive echoes of the past can be drowned out by the triumphant symphony of self-expression—with just a touch of humor to keep things interesting.

Blossom of Resilience

Picture a cityscape, the gritty streets of an inner city, a place where challenges loom as large as towering buildings. Ezekiel 7:10, a biblical declaration, echoes through this urban landscape: "Behold, the day, behold, it comes: your doom is gone forth; the rod has blossomed, pride has budded." In this environment, my story unfolds, a tale of resilience sprouting amid adversity, much like a determined flower pushing through the cracks in the concrete.

My mother, a resilient figure in her own right, understood the profound impact that surroundings and companionship could wield on an individual. She navigated the struggles of the ghetto with an unwavering spirit, recognizing the potential influence it could have on shaping one's character. Against adversity, she emerged as a guiding force, proving that the strength of one's character can triumph even in the harshest circumstances.

Our story plays out in the challenging terrain of a socially disadvantaged area, where many succumb to the opposing currents of their environment. Yet, armed with courage and determination, my mother charted a different course for me. She emphasized that resilience is a response to challenges and a proactive choice to rise above negativity.

In the refuge of extracurricular activities, our sanctuary from the struggles of the ghetto, music, dance, and drama became our escape hatch. Through these creative pursuits, a world beyond the limitations of our surroundings revealed itself. My mother's wisdom became a beacon, guiding us toward a different way of life—one defined by the pursuit of knowledge, cultural enrichment, and a broader perspective.

This section, set against the shadows of adversity, weaves a narrative akin to Ezekiel's blossoming rod, symbolizing the transformative power of a strong will and the nurturing influence of positive surroundings. Despite the challenges of growing up in the ghetto, the flowers of resilience and courage bloomed, breaking through the concrete of adversity and reaching for the sunlight of a brighter, more expansive future.

Imagine this story inspiring others, encouraging them to cultivate their blossoms in the face of adversity. For in the heart of every challenge lies the potential for remarkable growth and triumph. It's a reminder that, like a determined flower pushing through concrete, resilience can break through the most challenging circumstances and bloom into something beautiful.

Unveiling the Miracles

Envision life as a grand novel, each page adorned with verses echoing the profound declaration, "God is love," from 1 John 4:8. This section unfolds as the narrative delves into the intricate layers of my journey, revealing an embroidery woven with threads of pain, resilience, and the undeniable presence of miracles that grace the very fabric of existence. Hand in hand with God, I traverse valleys, ultimately guided toward the radiant light that leads to freedom.

Becoming a mother wasn't just another chapter; it marked a defining moment in my life's story. It unfolded like a captivating scene from a movie, revealing the profound truth that children are not only blessings but living miracles meticulously crafted by the hands of God. The revelation of my parentage, the trials endured in childbirth, and the complex dynamics of relationships deepened my appreciation for the profound essence of self-love.

Amid life's revelations, a pivotal moment emerged when the weight of the term *bastard* at birth became a catalyst, propelling me toward embracing the grander design within God's divine plan. This story unfolds further in an upcoming section titled "Two-Timing Tomfoolery," shedding light on my father's past. Picture the dance of life unfolding with unexpected turns, leading my parents full circle. The irony lies in my father's dependence on the very woman he had once mistreated, showcasing the intricate threads of divine intervention woven into our lives as I break free from those chains.

Through myriad challenges, a steadfast belief anchored me—the unwavering conviction that treating others with kindness, understanding, and love reflects the inherent beauty within us all. This section stands as a testament to the miracles that unfold when we embrace God's love, navigating life's intricate embroidery with resilience, gratitude, and an enduring appreciation for the miracles that grace our existence.

Life Lesson

The life lesson from this section is a call to embrace the valleys of life as opportunities for growth and transformation. It reminds us that even in our darkest moments, God's radiant light shines brightest, illuminating the path to freedom and renewal. As we journey onward, let us hold onto this truth, finding strength and purpose in every step we take toward the radiant light that leads to true freedom.

Freedom Notes

Embark on a transformative journey from stifled constraint to empowered liberation, guided by profound spiritual insights that illuminate the path ahead. Colossians 3:21 paints a poignant picture of a childhood suffocated by the oppressive mantra of "children should be seen and not heard," casting a heavy shadow over the budding sense of freedom within. Despite the weight of this environment, Ezekiel 7:10 reveals the emergence of resilience akin to a determined flower pushing through concrete cracks.

As the layers of my story unravel, illuminated by the divine truth of 1 John 4:8, they unveil a tapestry woven with threads of pain, resilience, and the miraculous presence of God intertwined within the fabric of existence. Hand in hand with the divine, traverse valleys and scale mountains, guided toward the radiant light of freedom that beckons from beyond.

Becoming a mother isn't merely another chapter; it marks a defining moment in the journey toward empowerment and self-discovery. With each step forward, embrace the transformative power of divine love and the boundless potential that awaits on the horizon. Let the story of liberation inspire others to embark on their own journeys of self-discovery, knowing that with faith as our guide, freedom is not merely a destination but a state of being to be embraced and celebrated.

_____

_____

_____

_____

_____

_____

_____

_____

_____

_____

_____

_____

_____

_____

_____

Workbook Section

Deep Reflections

- Prompt: Reflecting on the profound lesson of embracing love in its purest form, how do you perceive the concept of freedom within the intricately woven tapestry of life? As you navigate the threads of kindness, understanding, and love, how do you find liberation in recognizing and appreciating the divine beauty within yourself and others? Moreover, in acknowledging life's miracles and blessings, how does this awareness elevate your existence beyond the confines of your own story, opening the door to a more profound sense of freedom and connection?

Actionable Steps

1. Exploring the Concept of Freedom
   - Reflect: Contemplate what freedom means to you within the broader context of life's tapestry. How do love, kindness, and understanding play a role in your sense of freedom?
   - Write: Describe a moment when you experienced a profound sense of freedom through acts of love and kindness. How did this experience shift your perspective on freedom?

2. Journaling Exercise
   - Explore: Write about how recognizing and appreciating the divine beauty in yourself and others has affected your sense of liberation. How has this appreciation influenced your relationships and self-view?
   - Contemplate: Reflect on how acknowledging life's miracles and blessings has elevated your experience beyond your own story. How does this broader awareness contribute to a deeper sense of freedom?

3. Navigating the Threads of Life
   - Identify: Identify a specific area in your life where you feel constrained. How can kindness, understanding, and love help you navigate and transform this constraint into a space of freedom?
   - Act: Develop a plan to incorporate more acts of kindness and understanding in this area. How can these actions help you feel more liberated and connected?

4. Embracing Divine Beauty
   - Visualize: Picture yourself and others enveloped in a divine light that highlights your inherent beauty. How does this visualization affect your sense of freedom and self-worth?
   - Illustrate: Create a visual representation or written reflection that captures the divine beauty you see in yourself and others. How does this perspective enhance your feelings of freedom and connection?

5. Acknowledging Miracles and Blessings
   - Reflect: Take time to recognize and appreciate the miracles and blessings in your life. How does this awareness shift your focus from limitations to a broader sense of freedom?
   - Document: Keep a gratitude journal where you record daily miracles and blessings. Reflect on how this practice contributes to a more profound sense of freedom and connection.

6. Daily Affirmation
   - Write: Craft an affirmation that reflects your commitment to embracing love and recognizing divine beauty, such as "I embrace the freedom that comes from recognizing the divine beauty in myself and others, allowing love to guide my journey."
   - Repeat: Start each day by reciting this affirmation, reinforcing your commitment to freedom and connection through love and appreciation.

7. Reflection on Progress
    -   Monitor: At the end of each week, review how your understanding of freedom has evolved. How has embracing love and kindness influenced your sense of liberation?
    -   Adjust: Consider any adjustments needed in your approach to experiencing freedom and connection. What new steps can you take to deepen this understanding and practice?

Gifts

- A Tale of Generosity, Traditions, and Joyful Giving (Matthew 2:10–11)
- Celebrating Children as Life's Melodic Treasures (Psalm 127:3)

A Tale of Generosity, Traditions, and Joyful Giving

"WHEN THEY SAW THE STAR, THEY WERE OVERJOYED. ON COMING TO THE house, they saw the child with his mother, Mary, and they bowed down and worshiped him. Then they opened their treasures and presented him with gold, frankincense, and myrrh gifts" (Matthew 2:10–11). Growing up, Christmas for me was like winning the jackpot—you know, that feeling when you hit the jackpot on a game show and everything just falls into place? But instead of cash prizes, it was a whirlwind of gifts swirling around me like a snowstorm! And let me tell you, it wasn't just about the presents. It was a full-blown assault on the senses: twinkling lights turning the house into a fairy tale, ornaments shining like they were auditioning for a spot in the crown jewels, and enough tinsel to make even the most festive elves green with envy.

But amid all the glitter and cheer, there was a shadow lurking in the corners of our holiday festivities. You see, while my mom worked her magic to make Christmas a spectacle to behold, there was a sadness that hung over her like a stubborn cloud. She would share stories of her childhood, of being an orphan, of birthdays forgotten in the midst of Christmas chaos, and of feeling overlooked. It was like a sharp pinprick to the festive bubble we'd created.

Now, let's talk turkey—or rather, Christmas feast. My mom, bless her culinary skills, could whip up a spread fit for royalty. I'm talking about a feast so epic it could rival the banquet scenes from medieval movies. Picture tables sagging under the weight of roast turkeys, glazed hams, mountains of mashed potatoes, and rivers of gravy. It was enough to make even the most dedicated foodie weak at the knees.

However, at this juncture, events took an unexpected turn: my dad's yearly custom of welcoming strangers to share our dinner table. Yes, you heard that right—strangers off the street becoming part of our holiday shenanigans. As a child, I couldn't wrap my head around it. I mean, who invites random people to their Christmas feast? But Dad, with his heart of gold, saw it as an opportunity to spread a little cheer, even if it meant sacrificing a few extra slices of turkey.

As I grew older, I began to understand that Christmas wasn't just about the glitz and the glam, or even the mouthwatering feasts. It was about something deeper, something more profound. It was about reaching out to others, about sharing the warmth and joy of the season with those who needed it most. And so I made it my mission to carry on our family traditions, to keep the spirit of Christmas alive in my way.

Life Lesson

Amid the tinsel and the turkey, let's not forget the true meaning of Christmas. It's about more than just gifts and goodies; it's about spreading love and kindness wherever we go. Like the wise men who brought gifts to baby Jesus, we too can make the world a little brighter by sharing love with those around us. So let's keep the holiday spirit alive, not just during the festive season but every day of the year. After all, the greatest gift we can give is love, and by spreading love and cheer, we can make the world a little brighter, one act of kindness at a time. So let's embrace the magic of Christmas, and let's keep the spirit alive all year round!

Celebrating Children as Life's Melodic Treasures

Imagine the symphony of life, with the crescendo of divine blessings echoing harmonious notes from Psalm 127:3, declaring, "Children are a heritage from the LORD, offspring a reward from him." It's like being handed a ticket to the grandest show on Earth, with front-row seats reserved just for you. Have you ever felt the profound joy of offering something dearly cherished to the world or a stranger? This section in the embroidery of my life unfolds as a poetic ode to the most precious gifts bestowed upon me— my beloved children. They aren't just offspring; they are divine treasures, carrying within them the essence of grace and a purpose that transcends the confines of familial ties.

Picture a tender and intimate moment, like the warmth of a sunrise, as I reminisce about my son's baptism. It wasn't just a ceremony; it was a sacred event that became a heartfelt expression of gratitude and surrender. As the holy waters embraced him, I communed with the Creator, acknowledging that this child was not mine alone to possess. In a spiritual revelation, I understood that God had entrusted me with a sacred duty—to nurture, guide, and empower my children, sculpting them into compassionate and resilient beings.

The baptism, far more than a mere ritual, symbolized the act of returning this precious gift to the divine source from whence it came. It was like a cosmic handshake with God, sealing the pact that these children were lent to me for a purpose—to shape them into productive citizens, instill positive morals and values, foster social skills, and, above all, nurture their connection with God. The weight of this responsibility wasn't a burden but a divine calling, a calling that came with a divine guidebook filled with laughter, tears, and a sprinkle of humor.

As I navigated the intricate path of parenthood, I discovered that our children are not vessels of possession but of divine gifts. They are like little potential parcels wrapped in youth's curiosity. This realization became a guiding principle, compelling me to ensure that, upon completing the monumental task of upbringing, my children would be ready to step into the world, their inner light radiating brightly.

You see, the accurate measure of time lies in what we do with the gifts entrusted to us. Our children are not mere extensions of ourselves; they are entrusted to us as vessels of potential, purpose, and light. This section unfolds as a testament to the sacred journey of parenting, where the gifts bestowed by God are nurtured and cherished and eventually released into the world. Their radiance becomes a beacon of hope and inspiration for others, a symphony of gifts that continues to resonate through the shade of life.

Life Lesson

And so the life lesson that emerges from this section is akin to conducting a harmonious symphony. Embrace the divine gifts, nurture them with love and purpose, and let their unique melodies echo through the grand stage of life when the time comes. In doing so, you celebrate the essence of parenthood and contribute to the ongoing symphony of existence.

Gifts Notes

Delve into a heartwarming tale of generosity, tradition, and the boundless joy of giving, drawing inspiration from the timeless wisdom of Matthew 2:10–11. Reflecting on my childhood, Christmas emerged as a moment akin to striking a jackpot, with gifts cascading upon me like treasures from a grand game show. Yet, beyond the material abundance, it was a sensory extravaganza—twinkling lights casting a magical glow, ornaments shimmering like stars, and the enchanting allure of tinsel transforming our humble abode into a winter wonderland, all thanks to the artistic touch of my dear mother.

In the midst of this festive abundance, the gentle reminder of Psalm 127:3 resonates deeply within, highlighting the profound blessings bestowed upon us through the gift of children. They are not merely offspring but embodiments of grace, carrying within them a purpose that transcends familial ties. Their presence enriches every facet of life, weaving a poetic tribute in the very fabric of my existence.

As I journey through the memories of Christmases past, let us not only celebrate the tangible gifts exchanged but also the intangible blessings bestowed upon us by the presence of loved ones and the profound grace of God. May this reflection inspire us all to cherish the beauty of giving, to embrace the spirit of generosity, and to recognize the invaluable treasures that grace our lives each and every day.

_____
_____
_____
_____
_____
_____
_____
_____
_____
_____
_____
_____

Workbook Section

Deep Reflections

- Prompt: Reflecting on the symphony of life and the concept of gifts bestowed upon us, how do you perceive the role of nurturing and celebrating these divine blessings? As you navigate the grand stage of existence, how do you harmonize the unique melodies of your gifts with the ongoing symphony of life? Moreover, in embracing and celebrating your gifts, how do you contribute to the collective harmony of existence, ensuring that your melody resonates through the gifts God has bestowed upon you?

Actionable Steps

1. Understanding Your Gifts
   - Reflect: Contemplate the gifts and talents you believe have been bestowed upon you. How do these gifts contribute to your sense of purpose and fulfillment in life?
   - Write: Describe specific moments when you felt your gifts were particularly influential. How did nurturing and celebrating these gifts affect your experience?

2. Journaling Exercise
   - Explore: Write about how you currently nurture and celebrate your gifts. How does this process help you maintain a sense of connection and harmony in your life?
   - Contemplate: Reflect on ways you can further enhance your ability to harmonize your gifts with the ongoing symphony of life. What new practices can you implement?

3. Harmonizing Your Gifts
   - Identify: Identify areas in your life where your gifts could be better integrated or expressed. How can you align these gifts with the broader context of your life's purpose?
   - Act: Develop a plan for how you will bring your gifts into these areas, ensuring they contribute positively to your personal and collective harmony.

4. Celebrating Divine Blessings
   - Visualize: Imagine your gifts as unique melodies within the grand symphony of existence. How does this visualization affect your understanding of their role and significance?
   - Illustrate: Create a visual representation or written reflection on how celebrating your gifts enhances your life and contributes to the collective harmony. How does this celebration influence your interactions with others?

5. Contributing to Collective Harmony
   - Reflect: Consider how your gifts contribute to the collective harmony of existence. How do your actions and contributions resonate with the broader community or world?
   - Document: Write about ways you actively ensure your gifts are used for the greater good. What steps can you take to enhance this contribution?

6. Daily Affirmation
   - Write: Craft an affirmation that reflects your commitment to nurturing and celebrating your gifts, such as "I honor and celebrate the divine gifts bestowed upon me, harmonizing my unique melodies with the symphony of life."
   - Repeat: Recite this affirmation daily to reinforce your dedication to embracing and contributing your gifts.

7. Reflection on Progress

- Monitor: At the end of each week, review how your understanding and celebration of your gifts have evolved. How has this process affected your sense of purpose and connection?

- Adjust: Consider any adjustments needed to better integrate and celebrate your gifts. What new steps can you take to ensure your gifts contribute to the collective harmony?

Love

- Love, Laughter, and Two-Timing Tomfoolery (Matthew 5:44)
- The Compass of Love (1 Corinthians 16:14)

Love, Laughter, and Two-Timing Tomfoolery

"BUT I SAY UNTO YOU, LOVE YOUR ENEMIES, BLESS THEM THAT CURSE you, do good to them that hate you, and pray for them which despitefully use you, and persecute you" (Matthew 5:44). In the heart of Newark, where life unfolded like a captivating comedy, my family's story took the spotlight. Imagine a vibrant cityscape as the backdrop, a bustling city with a narrative written by the unexpected, and my parents, the starring duo in a play of love, laughter, and two-timing tomfoolery.

The tale started with a revelation worthy of a soap opera's grand reveal. Enter my dear old dad, the mastermind behind a stunning deception. He successfully duped my mom into believing they were living a happily married life while secretly juggling two matrimonial commitments. Cue the gasps and the laughter track—Mom unknowingly became the costar in a matrimonial sitcom, complete with a soundtrack of disbelief.

As a young woman processing this sitcom-level absurdity, I struggled to grasp the magnitude of it all. How on earth did Mom choose to stay after discovering she was living in a marital double feature? The man she believed she had exclusively turned out to have a backup spouse tucked away in some forgotten scene. It was a real-life soap opera, minus the glamorous sets and dramatic background music.

And then there was me, the unintentional offspring caught in the crossfire of my father's matrimonial mischief. Learning that I was technically a "bastard" child wasn't exactly a highlight in my childhood reel. But in the chaotic comedy of our lives, the unexpected consistently took center stage.

Amid the chaos, Mom's love held steadfast, a living testament to the mysterious agape love mentioned in Matthew 5:44. It was the kind of love that extended beyond betrayal, deception, and the jaw-dropping absurdity of two-timing tomfoolery. Mom, a resilient protagonist, decided to rewrite this topsy-turvy plot into a tale of redemption.

With a determination that would rival any superhero, Mom took on the Herculean task of helping Dad untangle his matrimonial mess. She navigated the bureaucratic maze, helped my dad through the process of filing for divorce from his first spouse, and, against all odds, aimed to turn her scripted life into something resembling a rom-com with a happy ending.

Yet, as an audience member thrust into this unexpected theater of the absurd, I harbored mixed feelings. While I admired Mom's strength and determination, I grappled with conflicting thoughts. I questioned the narrative I'd been raised on—the notions of love, loyalty, and how to respond when the script takes an unexpected turn.

The saga continued with an unexpected twist. Now without legs due to a cruel twist of fate, Dad became the invalid lead in this unconventional love story. Mom, undeterred by the challenges of caring for a man whose legs had become a casualty of life's harsh turns, continued to show her unwavering love. It was a unique kind of love, the agape kind, tested and refined in the crucible of life's absurdities.

As Mom tended to Dad's needs, enduring lies, deceit, and the limitations life had thrown away, I witnessed a love transcending conventionality. It was a love that laughed in the face of two-timing tomfoolery and emerged stronger, wiser, and undeniably real.

Life Lesson

Matthew 5:44 instructs us to love others with agape love, whether they are fellow believers or bitter enemies. Reflecting on love, I think of my mother—a woman who embodied agape love despite the two-timing tomfoolery and unexpected twists. In life's comedy, she taught me that true love persists through laughter, tears, and the absurdities of a two-timing tale. It also taught me the value of discernment, knowing when to let go, and safeguarding my heart from the heartbreak that accompanied deceit, unlike the resilience shown by my mom.

The Compass of Love

Picture this section of my life as a grand canvas, each stroke and hue representing the vibrant and intricate threads of love. At the core of my journey, the North Star guiding my steps is the timeless wisdom from 1 Corinthians 16:14, "Let all that you do be done in love." So let's dive into the embroidery of my experiences, a vivid portrait of the transformative power of love.

Relationships, my dear friends, are where love dons its golden robe and steps into the spotlight. It's the golden thread weaving through the fabric of connections, creating resilient bonds to withstand a tornado of challenges. This isn't just any love; it's a love that radiates from a divine source, an unconditional force shaping how I engage with my family, friends, and the vast world around me. Imagine joy amplified by love and sorrow, finding solace in its comforting embrace. It's a love that's both a shield and a warm blanket.

Let's talk about self-love, a profound odyssey that's a bit like finding the perfect pair of shoes. Love becomes the anchor, the sturdiest part of the ship, allowing me to navigate the stormy seas of personal growth. Love is the key to unlocking identity, acceptance, and self-discovery complexities in this quest. It's like having an eternal cheerleader reminding me that being perfectly imperfect is okay.

Parenthood, ah, the section dedicated to my little bundles of chaos and joy. Here, love takes on a superhero cape, a nurturing force that guides, protects, and empowers. Every word and action is a love letter written with the ink of unwavering commitment. It's a love that celebrates the uniqueness of each child, fostering a foundation built on love's enduring strength. It's like the magic wand that turns ordinary moments into extraordinary memories.

Let's swing by the realm of friendships. Love, my friends, is the foundation of authentic connections. It's a love that doesn't discriminate, embracing diversity, celebrating shared moments, and standing tall in the face of challenges. Love remains a constant through the roller coaster of companionship, creating a community where hearts intertwine with genuine care. It's like a garden where each friendship is a unique, blooming flower, adding color to the landscape of life.

In the whirlwind of life's challenges, when curveballs abound and obstacles rain down like confetti, the compass of love steadfastly guides my path. Rather than clutching onto grudges, love fosters empathy, understanding, and forgiveness. Each conflict becomes a stepping stone for personal growth, teaching me to recognize the shared humanity in others and embrace the beauty of reconciliation. It's akin to navigating the chapters of a story, where every plot twist imparts profound life lessons. Additionally, I've learned the value of loving from a distance when circumstances dictate, a lesson that has been instrumental in shaping my journey.

So, dear reader, I invite you to join me on this journey through the transformative landscapes of love. May the compass of love guide you in all you do, creating a symphony of kindness, compassion, and joy in the grand orchestration of life. And here's a nugget of wisdom from my experience: let love be your North Star, your guiding light. For in the tapestry of life, the threads of love create the most breathtaking masterpiece.

Love Notes

Embark with me on a captivating narrative journey brimming with love, laughter, and the intricate tapestry of human relationships, drawing inspiration from the profound teachings of Matthew 5:44. Against the dynamic backdrop of Newark's bustling cityscape, my family's story unfolds like a captivating comedy, with my parents as the endearing protagonists in a play of love, laughter, and unexpected plot twists.

Reflecting on the essence of love, my mother emerges as a shining beacon of agape love, gracefully navigating the trials of two-timing tomfoolery with unwavering grace and resilience. Her journey imparts invaluable lessons on discernment, resilience, and the enduring nature of true love amid life's unpredictable twists and turns.

Guided by the illuminating compass of love as described in 1 Corinthians 16:14, I traverse life's winding paths and unforeseen obstacles with empathy, understanding, and forgiveness. Each conflict becomes a catalyst for personal growth, fostering reconciliation and deepening my appreciation for the shared humanity in others.

Embrace the transformative landscapes of love as we journey together, inviting readers to join in this exploration. Let the compass of love orchestrate a symphony of kindness, compassion, and joy in their lives as we navigate the complexities of human connection and forge deeper bonds of understanding and empathy.

As I've learned through lived experience, let love serve as your guiding light, illuminating the path to a masterpiece of fulfillment and connection within the grand tapestry of life. Together, let us celebrate the transformative power of love and embrace its capacity to shape our lives with beauty, meaning, and profound connection.

_____

_____

_____

_____

_____

_____

_____

_____

_____

_____

_____

_____

_____

_____

Workbook Section

Deep Reflections

- Prompt: Considering the profound lesson of agape love illuminated by Matthew 5:44 and exemplified by the resilience of your mother or father, how do you navigate the complexities of love amid life's two-timing tales and unexpected twists? Reflecting on your experiences, how do you discern between genuine love and deceit, safeguarding your heart while embracing the enduring power of love to persist through laughter, tears, and absurdities? Moreover, how does your understanding of agape love shape your relationships with fellow believers or perceived enemies and guide you toward greater compassion and understanding?

Actionable Steps

1. Understanding Agape Love
   - Reflect: Contemplate the concept of agape love as described in Matthew 5:44. How do you understand this form of unconditional, selfless love? How does it compare to other forms of love you've experienced?
   - Write: Describe how the resilience of your mother or father exemplifies agape love. How has their example influenced your view on navigating love amid complexities?

2. Journaling Exercise
   - Explore: Write about a time when you had to navigate the complexities of love amid challenges. How did you discern between genuine love and deceit in this situation?
   - Contemplate: Reflect on how you protected your heart while maintaining a capacity to love. What strategies did you employ to ensure you embraced love's enduring power?

3. Navigating Love's Complexities
   - Identify: Identify a recent situation where you encountered two-timing tales or unexpected twists in a relationship. How did you handle these complexities while striving to remain true to agape love?
   - Act: Develop a plan for how you will approach similar situations in the future. What steps can you take to safeguard your heart while embracing the resilience and enduring power of love?

4. Discerning Genuine Love
   - Reflect: Reflect on your experiences of discernment in relationships. How have you learned to distinguish between genuine love and deceit?
   - Document: Write about how you have safeguarded your heart while maintaining the ability to embrace love through life's ups and downs. What insights have you gained from these experiences?

5. Shaping Relationships with Compassion
   - Explore: Consider how your understanding of agape love influences your relationships with fellow believers and perceived enemies. How does this perspective guide you toward greater compassion and understanding?
   - Illustrate: Create a visual or written representation of how agape love shapes your interactions and relationships. How does this influence your approach to others, especially those with whom you have conflicts?

6. Daily Affirmation
   - Write: Craft an affirmation that reflects your commitment to embracing agape love and navigating relationship complexities with compassion, such as "I embrace the enduring power of agape

love, navigating life's complexities with resilience, compassion, and understanding."

- Repeat: Recite this affirmation daily to reinforce your dedication to practicing and embodying agape love in your relationships.

7. Reflection on Progress
   - Monitor: At the end of each week, review how your understanding and practice of agape love have evolved. How has this affected your relationships and ability to navigate love amid complexities?
   - Adjust: Consider any adjustments needed in your approach to love and relationships. What new steps can you take to deepen your practice of agape love?

Marriage

- Matrimonial Chronicles (Hebrews 13:4)
- Harmony in the Broken Symphony (James 4:1–3)

Matrimonial Chronicles

IMAGINE THE EMBROIDERY OF LIFE UNFURLING ITS VIBRANT THREADS against the backdrop of divine guidance, as proclaimed in Hebrews 13:4, "Marriage should be honored by all, and the marriage bed kept pure, for God will judge the adulterer and all the sexually immoral." These words form the stage for the intricate tales of my life's journey through the realm of marriages—a section woven with threads of optimism, growth, turmoil, and, ultimately, profound lessons.

Embarking on the odyssey of my first marriage, I carried the radiant glow of optimism fueled by a sincere desire to wholeheartedly embrace my husband's dreams. From donning the hat of an assistant football coach to moonlighting as an assistant basketball coach and even trying my hand as an assistant radio host, I embraced roles that pushed me beyond the boundaries of my self-imposed limits. Despite the challenges that marked our journey, the experiences proved instrumental in my growth. Yet the shadows of abuse and turmoil loomed large, casting a pall over our successes. It became a stark reminder that losing oneself in pursuing a relationship could lead to tragic consequences. However, amid the storm, I found an unwavering anchor—my faith.

Vowing to approach my subsequent marriage with a different mindset, I set my sights on building a family and a future aligned with my vision. However, a haunting pattern emerged as I lost my identity in pursuing my husband's ambitions. As he aspired to become a pastor, a path divergent from my goals, the weight of responsibilities became overwhelming. Balancing roles such as critiquing sermons, developing curricula, leading church ministries, managing a household, fulfilling duties as a school leader, and raising three children became a Herculean task.

In the crucible of this relationship, stained by lies and deceit, I confronted a pivotal realization—I refused to be consumed by negativity. Drawing strength from the lessons embedded in the narrative of my parent's marriage, lessons I adamantly chose not to replicate, I made the courageous decision to break free and move forward. This section, etched with the complexities of love and loss, resilience, and revelation, is a testament to the transformative power of learning, growing, and daring to chart a course that aligns with the essence of one's being.

Through the peaks and valleys of these unions, I unearthed invaluable insights—lessons that transcended the conventional boundaries of love. Marriages, far beyond being mere unions of hearts, became profound crucibles of self-discovery and resilience. Each experience sculpted the contours of my character, molding me into a person who could weather storms and emerge with newfound wisdom. As I navigate the sections yet to be written, I carry the torch of these lessons, illuminating the path with the light of understanding, compassion, and the unwavering strength to honor the sanctity of love and self.

So, in the grand orchestration of life, let the strings of experience resonate with the melody of growth, and may the harmony of lessons learned guide you through the symphony of love and self-discovery. In honoring the sanctity of marriage and the sacredness of one's being, you unfurl a tapestry uniquely yours, a masterpiece woven with threads of resilience, understanding, and unwavering strength.

Harmony in the Broken Symphony

In the melodic verses of James 4:1–3, I uncovered a profound exploration of the human struggle for connection, entwined with the intricate dance of desires. "What causes fights and quarrels among you? Don't they come from your desires that battle within you?" These words became a guiding lantern, illuminating the path through the turbulent waters of broken connections and the relentless pursuit of wholeness.

Imagine the many facets of my life, a vibrant canvas interwoven with threads of joy and sorrow, unveiling a recurring motif: brokenness within the realm of companionship. Two husbands and potential mates, with hearts well intentioned yet unable to fathom the profound depth of my shattered soul, inadvertently contributed to the mosaic of my despair. The irony, bitter and sweet, lay in the realization that the one who could potentially understand was submerged in his sea of broken pieces.

Envision this cosmic play as a puzzle missing crucial parts or a symphony with a note mysteriously absent. My journey seeking companionship resembled attending a potluck with hopes of a grand feast, only to encounter a collection of mismatched snacks—a bag of chips, a lonely celery stick, and the inevitable leftover cheese cube. Hardly the soul-nourishing banquet envisaged.

In my relentless pursuit of filling the void, I stumbled, tripped, and sometimes face-planted into situations that only deepened the chasm within me. It felt akin to fixing a leaky boat with a sieve—a futile and exhausting endeavor.

Enter divine intervention. God, in His infinite wisdom, became my refuge and solace. Amid shattered connections and unmet expectations, His unwavering presence held me together when everything threatened to collapse. God, the glue, the healer of fractures that no human touch could mend.

Yet a persistent void lingered—not a flaw or imperfection but a space reserved for someone of complete wholeness. Picture a puzzle piece awaiting its perfect match—no forceful squeezing or reshaping required, just a seamless fit.

A profound realization surfaced: this void may never be filled by anyone. It demands a person who is physically present, mentally, spiritually, and wholly attuned to their being. It's an intricate and delicate dance requiring two complete partners, each embracing their wholeness.

So the lesson echoing through the corridors of my experience is crystal clear: do not rush the dance. Embrace your wholeness, allow others to find their completeness, and trust that the dance of connection will be harmonious and fulfilling when the time is right. After all, the most beautiful symphonies are composed of perfectly tuned notes, not rushed improvisations.

Marriage Notes

Step into the tapestry of my life's journey, where the threads of matrimonial bonds are intricately woven with the guiding wisdom of Hebrews 13:4. In this narrative, you'll discover an embroidery of optimism, growth, turmoil, and profound lessons, each experience resonating with the melody of personal development and self-discovery.

Honoring the sanctity of marriage and the sacredness of individual beings, I extend an invitation to unfurl your own tapestry, weaving a masterpiece of resilience, understanding, and unwavering strength. Together, let us embark on a journey of exploration and growth, where each thread represents a moment of transformation and revelation.

As we delve into the delicate dance of human connection depicted in James 4:1–3, we confront the intertwined desires and the quest for fulfillment. Through this exploration, a profound realization emerges: genuine connection flourishes when two complete partners, each embracing their wholeness, come together in harmony.

The lesson echoing through the corridors of my experience is clear: patience is paramount. Embrace personal wholeness, allowing others the space to find their completeness, and trust that genuine connection will manifest harmoniously in due time. For, as I've learned, the most beautiful symphonies of love are composed of perfectly tuned notes, not rushed improvisations. Let us embrace the journey of marriage with grace, understanding, and an unwavering commitment to growth, knowing that each moment holds the potential for profound transformation and deeper connection.

_____

_____

_____

_____

_____

_____

_____

_____

_____

_____

_____

_____

_____

_____

Workbook Section

Deep Reflections

- Prompt: Reflecting on the symphony of love and self-discovery within marriage, how do you perceive the interplay between honoring the sanctity of union and embracing individual completeness? Drawing from the lessons of resilience, understanding, and unwavering strength, how do you navigate the journey of marriage as a tapestry uniquely woven with shared experiences and personal growth? Moreover, when considering the tempo of connection, how do you balance patience to allow for harmonious alignment with the desire for fulfillment, recognizing that the most beautiful symphonies are composed of perfectly tuned notes, not rushed improvisations?

Actionable Steps

1. Honoring Union and Embracing Individuality
    -   Reflect: Contemplate how you balance honoring the sanctity of marriage with maintaining your sense of individual completeness. How do you honor both the union and your personal growth?
    -   Write: Describe a specific example where you successfully navigated the balance between togetherness and individuality in your marriage. How did this experience affect your relationship?

2. Journaling Exercise
    -   Explore: Write about how resilience, understanding, and unwavering strength play a role in your marriage. How have these qualities helped you navigate challenges and grow together?
    -   Contemplate: Reflect on your personal growth within the marriage. How has your journey of self-discovery influenced your relationship?

3. Navigating Shared Experiences and Growth
   - Identify: Identify key shared experiences that have shaped your marriage. How do these experiences contribute to the tapestry of your relationship?
   - Act: Develop a plan for continuing to weave new shared experiences into your marriage while also nurturing your personal growth. What steps can you take to enrich your journey together?

4. Balancing Connection and Fulfillment
   - Reflect: Consider how you balance the desire for fulfillment with the need for patience in your marriage. How does this balance affect the harmony and growth of your relationship?
   - Document: Write about how you manage the tempo of connection and patience. How does this approach contribute to a harmonious and fulfilling relationship?

5. Creating a Symphony of Marriage
   - Visualize: Imagine your marriage as a symphony, with each partner contributing unique notes to the composition. How do you ensure that the symphony is composed of perfectly tuned notes rather than rushed improvisations?
   - Illustrate: Create a visual or written representation of how you and your partner contribute to this symphony. How do you work together to achieve harmony and fulfillment?

6. Daily Affirmation
   - Write: Craft an affirmation that reflects your commitment to both honoring the sanctity of your union and embracing personal growth, such as "I honor the sacred bond of marriage while nurturing my individual growth, creating a harmonious symphony through patience and understanding."

- Repeat: Recite this affirmation daily to reinforce your dedication to balancing connection and personal fulfillment within your marriage.

7. Reflection on Progress
   - Monitor: At the end of each week, review how your understanding and practice of balancing union and individuality have evolved. How has this affected the harmony and growth in your marriage?
   - Adjust: Consider any adjustments needed in your approach to balancing connection and personal fulfillment. What new steps can you take to continue enriching your marriage?

Balance

- Navigating the Tightrope of Wealth and Temptation (1 Timothy 6:9–10)
- Navigating Work and Life Harmony (Ecclesiastes 3:1)
- A Journey Home to Self-Discovery (James 1:22–25)

Navigating the Tightrope of Wealth and Temptation

"THOSE WHO WANT TO GET RICH FALL INTO TEMPTATION AND A TRAP and into many foolish and harmful desires that plunge people into ruin and destruction" (1 Timothy 6:9–10). Growing up, my parents danced on the tightrope between comfort and chaos like seasoned performers in a circus act. They were what you might call middle-class warriors, hustling day in and day out to provide for our family. But here's the kicker—they weren't just about the nine-to-five grind. Oh no, they had a taste for the finer things in life, and they weren't afraid to indulge.

Now, picture this: a typical evening at our house, the lights flickering ominously because Dad had rolled the dice once too often. Yup, you heard it right—gambling was his guilty pleasure, his ticket to a roller-coaster ride of highs and lows. And let me tell you, it wasn't always a smooth ride. I can still feel the knot in my stomach as Mom whispered in my ear, urging me to give Dad a gentle nudge during his poker games. Why? Well, let's just say it wasn't to wish him good luck. It was her way of trying to salvage what was left of his paycheck before it vanished into the abyss of the crap game.

Talk about a plot twist, right? Here I was, a wide-eyed child caught in the crossfire of my parents' high-stakes drama. It was like being handed a front-row ticket to the wildest show in town, with no intermission in sight. And in the midst of it all, I couldn't help but wonder—why on earth was Mom dragging me into her high-stakes game of financial roulette?

But you know what they say—every cloud has a silver lining. That roller-coaster ride through the ups and downs of my parents' financial adventures left an indelible mark on me. It was like a crash course in money management, with a side of emotional turmoil thrown in for good measure.

And you know what lesson I walked away with? A vow never to let a single penny slip through my fingers on the spin of a roulette wheel.

Life Lesson

So here's the deal, folks. Money might make the world go round, but it can also send you spinning out of control faster than you can say, "Jackpot." As tempting as it may be to chase after riches, heed the warning signs flashing in neon lights. Don't let the allure of easy money lead you down a path of ruin and destruction. Instead, tread carefully, and remember that true wealth lies not in material possessions but in the richness of love, family, and the simple joys of life. So let's steer clear of the traps and temptations that lurk in the shadows, and forge a path toward a brighter, more fulfilling future. After all, as the saying goes, it's not about the cards you're dealt but how you play the hand.

Navigating Work and Life Harmony

In the intricate dance of life, Ecclesiastes 3:1 gently whispered, "For everything, there is a season and a time for every matter under heaven." Little did I know this biblical wisdom would become my compass in navigating the delicate ballet between work and personal life. Imagine if my work had an all-access pass to every nook and cranny of my existence. It was like having an uninvited guest at a dinner party—always there, always lurking, and always ready to pounce on any moment of peace. My personal life felt like a neglected garden, overrun by the weeds of deadlines and the demanding whispers of the professional realm.

But fret not, dear reader, for in this tale, I found the magical elixir to restore the equilibrium—the elusive art of work-life balance. It was as if Ecclesiastes himself took me by the hand and led me to the revelation that harmony is not just a word but a state of being.

Picture this: my office, a bustling hive of productivity, transformed into a sanctuary of serenity as I learned to draw a boundary line between professional duties and personal bliss. It was like installing a velvet rope between two distinct realms, signaling to the stress and deadlines that they were not invited to the after-hours party.

I had to chuckle at the realization that my work, though a significant part of my life, was not entitled to a 24/7 VIP pass. It was time to cut it loose at the office door and let my personal life reclaim the spotlight. After all, even Cinderella had to leave the ball at midnight.

And then there were my friends, the unsung heroes in my pursuit of balance. We decided to have a little chat, and by "little chat," I mean a heart-to-heart conversation where I laid down the ground rules for our gatherings. No more work talk dominating the stage; it was time for a script change. I craved discussions about family escapades, personal goals, and the dreams that danced in the secret corners of our hearts.

Oh, the freedom! Work-related stress was banished to the shadows as we clinked glasses and savored the camaraderie. We created our haven, a space where the strains of professional life dared not intrude. It was liberating to share laughter and tales of personal triumphs without the looming specter of deadlines.

Life Lesson

Let me share the golden nugget gleaned from this adventure: much like a well-coordinated dance, life requires balance. Ecclesiastes 3:1 is a philosophical musing and a practical guide to reclaiming sanity. The lesson here is simple but profound—there is a time for everything, including work, play, and everything in between.

So, dear reader, let Ecclesiastes be your dance instructor in the grand ballroom of life. Establish those boundaries, prioritize the rhythm of your personal life, and let work know it can take a bow after its designated time on the stage. In this harmonious blend, you'll discover the beauty of balance, the joy of shared moments, and the timeless truth that every season has its unique dance.

A Journey Home to Self-Discovery

"Do not merely listen to the word, and so deceive yourselves. Do what it says. Anyone who listens to the word but does not do what it says is like someone who looks at his face in a mirror and, after looking at himself, goes away and immediately forgets what he looks like. But whoever looks intently into the perfect law that gives freedom, and continues in it—not forgetting what they have heard, but doing it—they will be blessed in what they do." James 1:22–25 serves as a gentle reminder that God's Word is a mirror, reflecting our progress, flaws, and the areas where growth is essential. In this divine reflection, my journey unfolds—a transformative tale sparked by the complexities of a challenging second marriage and the pursuit of inner peace, navigating through the uncharted territories meticulously crafted by God's hands.

Imagine the scene: a weary traveler, me, returning to the familiar grounds of the home, not just as a physical relocation but as a profound quest for self-discovery. The shadows of the challenging second marriage slowly dissipated; I carried an unwavering optimism, a beacon lighting the way on this unknown path.

Choosing to surround myself in the comforting familiarity of my mother's home, I soon realized that even the most familiar grounds could harbor unforeseen challenges. The sanctuary I sought was enveloped in turbulence, unpredictability, and an undercurrent of resentment within the unique, often complex, relationship with my mother. The weight of relentless expectations and the perpetual feeling of never measuring up created a stifling atmosphere, echoing the childhood pressures of attaining unattainable perfection. It was crystal clear—I couldn't thrive under the shadow of such control, especially with my precious children in tow.

Amid this tumult, an unexpected beacon of joy and peace emerged from cycling. Picture this, the rhythmic rotation of pedals beneath my feet and weaving a path toward reclaiming my identity. As I cycled through the twists and turns of the streets, the wind whispering tales of liberation, I found solace. Every push of the pedal became a declaration of independence, each revolution a symbolic gesture of breaking free from the constraints of my mother's influence.

The bicycle, more than a mode of transportation, became a symbolic vehicle for navigating the landscapes of my emotions. In its freedom, I sought a New Haven—a home unbound by the constrictions of familial expectations. Pursuing a harmonious life for my children and I unfolded with each turn of the bicycle wheels, a tangible manifestation of the freedom I craved.

This section weaves the transformative power of self-discovery through cycling, transcending the physical act of moving to symbolize a journey toward liberation. It's a testament to the resilience to seek one's path, even when navigating the challenging terrains of familial expectations. The bicycle's wheels not only turned through the streets but also turned the wheels of change in my life, propelling me toward a new section. In this section, I could rediscover, redefine, and rejoice in the authenticity of my existence.

In the symphony of life, may you find the rhythm that resonates with your heart and the balance that soothes your soul. Just like a skilled cyclist maintains equilibrium while navigating varied terrain, pedal toward the liberation that awaits your unique journey. Embrace the unexpected twists and turns, for in navigating these, you unveil the extraordinary resilience that lies within.

Balance Notes

Embark with me on a journey of profound self-discovery and resilience, guided by the timeless wisdom encapsulated in 1 Timothy 6:9–10. This scripture serves as a beacon, illuminating the path toward navigating life's myriad pitfalls and temptations. It reminds us to steer clear of the shadows where traps await, urging us to forge ahead toward a future brimming with brightness and fulfillment. Just as the adage suggests, life isn't solely about the cards we're dealt but rather how we choose to play them. This profound wisdom encourages us to take charge of our circumstances, shaping our destinies with resolve and purpose.

Delve into the intricate dance between work and personal life, guided by the transformative insights of Ecclesiastes 3:1. Through my own experiences, I've witnessed how the demands of work can sometimes overshadow the harmony of our personal lives, disrupting the delicate balance we strive to maintain. Yet, amid this journey, I've learned the invaluable lesson of establishing boundaries and prioritizing the rhythm of my personal life. By granting each aspect of life its rightful time on the stage, I've discovered the profound beauty of balance and the sheer joy of shared moments. It's a realization that each season holds its unique dance, and by embracing this truth, we can find solace amid life's ever-changing rhythms.

Inspired by the teachings of James 1:22–25, I've embarked on a deeply introspective journey fueled by the challenges of a second marriage and the quest for inner peace. God's Word acts as a mirror, reflecting my growth, vulnerabilities, and areas for further development. It serves as a poignant reminder that self-reflection and introspection are indispensable components of personal evolution. As I navigate the complexities of existence, I extend a heartfelt invitation for readers to join me on this transformative odyssey. Together, let us seek out the rhythm and equilibrium that soothe our souls, akin to a skilled cyclist maintaining balance amid varied terrain. May we embrace life's twists and turns as opportunities to unveil the extraordinary resilience within, pedaling toward liberation and fulfillment with unwavering determination.

_____

_____

_____

_____

_____

_____

_____

_____

_____

_____

_____

_____

Workbook Section

Deep Reflections

- Prompt: Reflecting on the allure and dangers of gambling or other vices, what steps can you take to resist the temptation of easy riches and instead cultivate a sense of fulfillment and contentment with your life? Contemplating the dance of life illuminated by Ecclesiastes, how do you establish boundaries and prioritize the rhythm of your personal and professional spheres to achieve a harmonious blend? Considering the beauty of balance and the joy of shared moments, how do you navigate the seasons of life, recognizing that each holds its unique dance? Moreover, as you pedal toward liberation and embrace the twists and turns of your journey, how do you unveil the extraordinary resilience within, finding the rhythm that resonates with your heart amid the symphony of life?

Actionable Steps

1. Resisting Temptations and Cultivating Fulfillment
   - Reflect: Contemplate the allure of gambling or other vices and how they promise easy riches. What temptations have you faced, and how have they affected your sense of fulfillment?
   - Write: Describe the steps you can take to resist these temptations and instead cultivate contentment in your life. What strategies can you implement to enhance your sense of fulfillment?

2. Journaling Exercise
   - Explore: Write about how you can apply the wisdom from Ecclesiastes to establish boundaries between personal and professional life. How do you plan to prioritize and maintain a harmonious blend?
   - Contemplate: Reflect on the rhythm of your life and how you can create a balanced approach to managing your responsibilities and passions.

3. Establishing Boundaries and Prioritizing Rhythm
   - Identify: Identify specific areas where boundaries are needed to achieve a better balance between personal and professional spheres. What steps will you take to set and maintain these boundaries?
   - Act: Develop a plan for prioritizing your responsibilities and activities to maintain a harmonious rhythm in your life. How will you ensure that each sphere of your life gets the attention it needs?

4. Navigating Life's Seasons
   - Reflect: Consider the different seasons of your life and how each one offers its own unique dance. How do you adapt to these changes and find joy in each phase?
   - Document: Write about how you navigate the transitions between different seasons and how you embrace the beauty of each stage.

5. Unveiling Resilience and Finding Rhythm
   - Explore: Reflect on the extraordinary resilience within you as you navigate the twists and turns of your journey. How do you find the rhythm that resonates with your heart amid life's challenges?
   - Illustrate: Create a visual or written representation of your journey toward liberation and balance. How does this rhythm align with your personal values and goals?

6. Daily Affirmation
   - Write: Craft an affirmation that reflects your commitment to resisting temptations, establishing boundaries, and embracing balance, such as "I cultivate fulfillment and contentment by resisting temptation, establishing harmonious boundaries, and embracing the unique rhythm of each season of life."
   - Repeat: Recite this affirmation daily to reinforce your dedication to maintaining balance and resilience in your life.

7. Reflection on Progress
   - Monitor: At the end of each week, review how your understanding and practice of balance have evolved. How has this affected your sense of fulfillment and harmony?
   - Adjust: Consider any adjustments needed in your approach to achieving balance. What new steps can you take to continue refining your sense of rhythm and resilience?

Grief

- Shadows of Loss (Matthew 5:4)
- Silent Wounds (Psalm 34:18)

Shadows of Loss—Navigating Grief, Finding Light

IN THE HALLOWED VERSES OF MATTHEW 5:4, THE DIVINE PROMISE RINGS out: "Blessed are those who mourn, for they shall be comforted." Yet, as I plunged into the depths of grief, I discovered how discomforting this roller-coaster journey truly could be. Once a source of solace and reassurance, the words of scripture now felt like distant echoes in the vast expanse of my sorrow.

Welcome to the most challenging chapter of my life, where the spotlight shines on the profound loss of my mother. Our relationship? Picture a roller-coaster ride through a carnival of emotions, with highs, lows, and unexpected loops—an intricate dance that spoke volumes of her unconventional love for me. When she exited the stage, I found myself in a moment of reflection, bravely confronting the complexities of our bond head-on.

Her absence played a whimsical tune on the strings of my heart. While I had mourned the loss of my father over a decade ago (cue the sentimental music), my mother's departure decided to play a game of hide-and-seek with my emotions. Shadows of grief came and went like waves at high tide, tossing me about in a sea of uncertainty.

Engage with me if you would about perceived shortcomings—those embarrassing dance moves we wish we could erase from memory. Mine were like colorful confetti scattered across the floor, a testament to the depth of our connection, quirks and all. The weight of loss, though heavy, became a catalyst for personal growth. It was as if the universe handed me a challenge, daring me to become the deluxe version of myself. Inspired by my mother's determination (and maybe a dash of stubbornness), I embarked on a journey of self-improvement, determined to outshine my limitations.

Digging into my mother's past was like excavating a treasure trove of untold stories. She wasn't just a character in the sitcom of my life; she had her own spin-off series. Her journey through orphanages and searches for family roots unveiled layers of pain and longing, flooding me with profound sorrow for her struggles. That's when I rolled up my sleeves and decided, "You know what? Time to confront my inner demons and show them who's boss."

Amid my mother's search for a sense of belonging, a surprising twist occurred after her death—I discovered she had a half brother. This unexpected revelation, which seemed almost like fate, provided a rare chance to strengthen my bond with her. Raised as an orphan, my mother felt a strong connection to her heritage, leading her on a moving journey through DNA tests and ancestry searches to uncover her roots. But the story took an unforeseen turn following her passing when I came across a remarkable revelation—her half brother, who just so happened to have a daughter named Shana, coincidentally sharing my name.

The irony of this chance discovery deeply affected me, offering a special opportunity to connect with my mother on a deeper level. However, the significance of this revelation was not lost on me. As I learned more about her struggles in seeking out family, I couldn't help but feel the weight of her hardships. Understanding the challenges she faced in trying to piece together her family history and the disappointment I experienced in my attempts to gather information from her half brother left a heavy burden on my heart.

Yet, amid the whirlwind of emotions, there was a profound sense of peace. Knowing that my mother no longer had to endure the arduous journey of seeking her roots brought bittersweet solace. In uncovering this piece of her past, I felt as though I could finally lay to rest the unanswered questions that had plagued her throughout her life.

In the end, this unexpected twist served as a poignant reminder of the resilience of the human spirit and the profound effect of familial bonds. Despite the challenges and disappointments, there is beauty in the journey of self-discovery and belonging—a journey that my mother embarked on with unwavering determination and that I now carry forward in her memory.

So, dear reader, fasten your seat belt and join me on this wild ride as we navigate the complexities of loss, move through the shadows, and search for the light that brightens the intricate tapestry of life. It's a journey that doesn't shy away from pain but also embraces those moments of joy—an exploration of grief, darkness, and the eternal pursuit of light. I'm learning to navigate and live through these emotions of grief, not suppressing them but riding the roller coaster of life with grace, embracing the twists and turns along the way.

Life Lesson

"Blessed are those who mourn." In the roller coaster of life, mourning is a part of the ride. But within the twists and turns, you'll find unexpected laughter, moments of joy, and the comforting light that guides you through the shadows. So embrace the ride, acknowledge the pain, and let the pursuit of light be your constant companion.

Silent Wounds (Psalm 34:18)

Silent Wounds—Navigating Grief, Finding Forgiveness

In the tender embrace of Psalm 34:18, we find a beautiful promise: "The Lord is close to the brokenhearted and saves those who are crushed in spirit." These words resonate within me like a comforting lullaby, especially during moments when my heart feels like it's doing a marathon through a minefield of anguish and regret.

Let's take a stroll down the winding path of my life, where the shadows of loss loom large. One of the heaviest burdens I carry is the emotional pain of having had an abortion—a chapter in my story that weighs down my spirit like a lead balloon. Imagine trying to float in a hot air balloon while lugging around a sack of bricks; that's what this wound feels like.

The decision was made in a chaotic whirlwind of turmoil, and now it feels like I'm living with a ghost—the ghost of a life that never had a chance to bloom. It haunts me like a catchy tune you can't get out of your head, playing on repeat long after the music has stopped. The echoes of that choice ripple through my life, and while the world continues to spin like a top, my soul is caught in the gravitational pull of regret.

This grief isn't unlike the profound sorrow I felt with the loss of my parents. It's a unique blend—grief for the child who never got to take a breath, grief for the version of myself who made that choice, and grief for the never-ending sense of remorse that feels like a shadow whispering in my ear. I remember that day vividly, wrapped in feelings of isolation, fear, and regret, which have woven themselves into the very fabric of my grief journey, making it nearly impossible to escape their grip.

I know, deep down, that God offers forgiveness, but the road to forgiving myself has been more like navigating a maze with a blindfold on—full of twists, turns, and the occasional wall that knocks the wind out of me. The internal chaos feels like a storm at sea, an unyielding tempest that leaves me questioning my worth and purpose. Yet, as I meditate on Psalm 34:18, I catch a glimmer of hope—like a lighthouse cutting through fog. God remains close to the brokenhearted, and though my spirit feels crushed, I lean into His embrace, reassured that even in my darkest hours, I am not alone.

This chapter has become an indelible part of my narrative—a testament to the complexities of healing. It's not a simple story with neat resolutions or easy answers. Instead, I'm learning that grief—whether born from loss, regret, or heartache—can serve as a pathway to understanding, growth, and transformation. It's a bit like tending a garden; sometimes, you must dig up the weeds before you can plant something beautiful.

So, as I navigate through these shadows of loss, I cling to the belief that with time and faith, light will eventually seep through the cracks, illuminating the path ahead.

Life Lesson

Grief comes in many forms, often stemming from the choices we've made. But even in our darkest moments, God's presence is unwavering. The journey toward self-forgiveness may be long and filled with obstacles, but it's also a path where God meets us with grace, ready to heal our broken hearts. It's a dance of sorts—sometimes clumsy, sometimes graceful, but always moving toward healing. And perhaps, just perhaps, a sprinkle of humor can help us see that even in grief, life goes on. So let's share a laugh while we navigate the ups and downs, because if we can find joy in the cracks, maybe we can learn to thrive amidst the silent wounds.

Grief Notes

Step into the depths of my soul as I navigate the turbulent waters of loss and despair, drawing solace from the timeless wisdom encapsulated in Ephesians 6:1–3. The passing of my mother plunged me into an abyss of grief, leaving me to grapple with the daunting task of arranging her funeral without her guiding presence by my side. In those harrowing moments, the comforting words of scripture felt like distant echoes amid the overwhelming weight of sorrow.

Together, let us embark on this raw and poignant journey through the complexities of loss as we navigate the shadows in search of the flickering light that illuminates life's intricate tapestry. This expedition doesn't shy away from the depths of pain but also embraces fleeting moments of joy—a testament to the human spirit's resilience in the face of adversity.

Through this profound experience, I am learning to navigate the turbulent emotions of grief with grace, riding the roller coaster of life and embracing its twists and turns along the way. Join me in unraveling the layers of sorrow and discovering the profound lessons hidden within as we emerge from the darkness with newfound understanding, resilience, and an unwavering faith in the journey ahead.

_____

_____

_____

_____

_____

_____

_____

_____

_____

_____

_____

_____

_____

Workbook Section

Deep Reflections

- Prompt: Reflecting on the roller coaster of life and the inevitability of mourning, how do you navigate grief amid unexpected moments of laughter and joy? Considering the comforting light that guides us through the shadows, how do you embrace the ride of life while acknowledging the pain of loss? Moreover, in the pursuit of light as a constant companion, how do you find solace and resilience amid the twists and turns of grief's journey?

Actionable Steps

1. Navigating Grief amid Joy
   - Reflect: Contemplate how grief and moments of joy coexist in your life. How do you navigate the complex emotions of mourning while still experiencing laughter and happiness?
   - Write: Describe a situation where you experienced grief alongside moments of joy. How did you manage these conflicting emotions, and what insights did you gain from this experience?

2. Journaling Exercise
   - Explore: Write about how the inevitability of mourning affects your daily life. How do you balance acknowledging the pain of loss with embracing moments of joy?
   - Contemplate: Reflect on how you can allow yourself to experience both grief and joy without feeling conflicted. What practices help you integrate these emotions into your life?

3. Embracing Life's Ride
   - Identify: Identify ways in which you can embrace the ride of life, even as you face the pain of loss. How can you acknowledge

and honor your grief while continuing to engage with life's experiences?

- Act: Develop a plan for incorporating practices that help you remain engaged with life's joys and challenges while navigating grief. What steps can you take to find balance?

4. Finding Solace and Resilience
   - Reflect: Consider the comforting light that guides you through the shadows of grief. How do you find solace and resilience amid the challenges of mourning?
   - Document: Write about sources of comfort and strength that help you navigate the twists and turns of grief. How do these sources support your journey?

5. Pursuit of Light and Resilience
   - Explore: Reflect on how the pursuit of light, or hope and positivity, serves as a constant companion in your journey through grief. How does this light guide you through the darker moments?
   - Illustrate: Create a visual or written representation of how you seek and find light amid your grief. How does this pursuit influence your ability to cope and heal?

6. Daily Affirmation
   - Write: Craft an affirmation that reflects your commitment to finding balance between grief and joy, and seeking solace and resilience, such as "I navigate the roller coaster of life with grace, embracing both grief and joy while finding comfort and resilience in the light that guides me."
   - Repeat: Recite this affirmation daily to reinforce your dedication to balancing grief with moments of joy and seeking solace in the journey.

7. Reflection on Progress

   - Monitor: At the end of each week, review how your understanding and practice of navigating grief have evolved. How has this affected your ability to find joy and solace amid mourning?

   - Adjust: Consider any adjustments needed in your approach to dealing with grief. What new steps can you take to continue finding resilience and light in your journey?

Finding Home

- Beyond Borders: Discovering My Forever Home (Psalm 127:1)

Beyond Borders: Discovering My Forever Home

"UNLESS THE LORD BUILDS THE HOUSE, THE BUILDERS LABOR IN VAIN. Unless the Lord watches over the city, the guards stand watch in vain" (Psalm 127:1). In the symphony of my upbringing, my parents didn't just raise me; they composed a masterpiece of travel experiences, leaving a legacy that resonates eternally within me. At first, these journeys felt like orchestrated obligations—packed bags, plane rides, and meticulously planned itineraries, courtesy of my mother's unwavering precision. Yet, as time wove its intricate embroidery, these expeditions transformed into portals of understanding, each trip unfolding like a divine revelation, guiding me toward a life beyond the familiar horizons of my upbringing.

Picture this: a young me, reluctantly dragging my feet onto planes, unaware that these moments of frustration were the prelude to a symphony of self-discovery. Through the kaleidoscope of travel, I discerned God's subtle hand orchestrating a destiny beyond the boundaries of my childhood community. Mundane excursions evolved into gateways of enlightenment, exposing me to the diverse shades of cultures, people, and experiences awaiting exploration.

Amid the enchantment of these adventures, a seed of desire sprouted—an aspiration for my forever home to transcend borders and find its anchor in a foreign land. The rhythmic heartbeat of life beyond my homeland became a wellspring of solace. The sun's warmth, sandy beaches, and the genuine kindness of unfamiliar faces spoke to my soul in this sanctuary. Each foreign destination left an indelible mark, stirring a profound longing for a place that harmonized with the cadence of my very being.

Embark with me on a transcendent journey beyond the United States, where the quest for my forever home unfolds against the canvas of diverse cultures and unfamiliar landscapes. It's not just a geographical exploration;

it's a narrative of self-discovery, a pilgrimage for peace and solace that led me to the profound realization that the coordinates of home are not confined to a single spot on the map. Instead, home is discovered in the embrace of foreign shores, under the open skies of distant lands, where the heart resonates and the spirit finds its belonging.

As we navigate through this section, let's revel in the humor of my early reluctance, appreciate the vivid colors of each cultural embroidery woven into my story, and find inspiration in the idea that home is not just a place but a feeling. This lesson transcends borders and encourages us to explore, connect, and discover the myriad homes awaiting us in this beautiful world's vast expanse.

Finding Home Notes

Embark with me on a soul-stirring expedition as we uncover the essence of finding my forever home, drawing inspiration from the timeless verses of Psalm 127:1. Raised by parents whose passion for travel was as boundless as the horizon, I initially regarded our journeys as obligatory escapades, meticulously orchestrated by my mother's precision.

Yet, with the passage of time, these expeditions metamorphosed into transformative odysseys of self-discovery. Each voyage became a sacred pilgrimage, offering profound insights that transcended the mere exploration of geographical terrains. As we traverse through this narrative, we'll share lighthearted chuckles at my early reluctance, marvel at the kaleidoscope of vibrant cultural encounters intricately woven into the fabric of my story, and contemplate the profound truth that home transcends the confines of physical boundaries—it's a sensation, an emotion that resonates within.

This lesson extends an invitation to explore, connect, and unravel the myriad homes awaiting us in the expansive canvas of this magnificent world. Let us journey together, guided by the whispers of our souls, as we uncover the true essence of home amid the boundless expanse of existence.

Shana Marie Burnett

_____

_____

_____

_____

_____

_____

_____

_____

_____

_____

_____

_____

_____

_____

_____

Workbook Section

Deep Reflections

- Prompt: Reflecting on the journey through the vivid colors of cultural embroidery woven into your story, how do you define the concept of *home* beyond its physical boundaries? Considering the lesson that home is not just a place but a feeling, how do you navigate the exploration and connection to the myriad homes awaiting in the vast expanse of the world? Moreover, how do you find inspiration in transcending borders to discover the true essence of *home* within yourself and the connections you cultivate?

Actionable Steps

1. Defining Home beyond Physical Boundaries
   - Reflect: Contemplate what *home* means to you beyond just a physical space. How do you experience *home* through your cultural, emotional, and relational connections?
   - Write: Describe how your understanding of *home* has evolved over time. What aspects of your journey have contributed to this broader definition?

2. Journaling Exercise
   - Explore: Write about different places or experiences where you have felt a strong sense of home. How did these experiences shape your view of what constitutes *home*?
   - Contemplate: Reflect on how the concept of home as a feeling rather than a place influences your daily life and relationships.

3. Navigating Exploration and Connection
   - Identify: Identify the various homes you have encountered in your life, whether cultural, emotional, or relational. How do these experiences contribute to your understanding of *home*?

- Act: Develop a plan for exploring and connecting with new homes or communities. How can you cultivate meaningful connections that align with your sense of home?

4. Finding Inspiration in Transcending Borders
   - Reflect: Consider how transcending physical and cultural borders has helped you discover the essence of home within yourself. How does this expanded perspective influence your sense of belonging?
   - Document: Write about instances where crossing borders—whether literal or metaphorical—has led to new insights about home. How has this inspired you to connect more deeply with yourself and others?

5. Discovering the Essence of Home
   - Explore: Reflect on how you can find and nurture the essence of home within yourself. What practices or habits help you cultivate a sense of belonging and comfort, regardless of your location?
   - Illustrate: Create a visual or written representation of the elements that contribute to your sense of home. How do these elements help you feel grounded and connected?

6. Daily Affirmation
   - Write: Craft an affirmation that reflects your journey in discovering and nurturing the true essence of home, such as "I find and create a sense of home through the connections I cultivate, the cultural richness I embrace, and the essence I carry within myself."
   - Repeat: Recite this affirmation daily to reinforce your commitment to exploring and cultivating a profound sense of home.

7. Reflection on Progress
    - Monitor: At the end of each week, review how your understanding and experience of *home* have evolved. How has this affected your sense of belonging and connection?
    - Adjust: Consider any adjustments needed in your approach to finding and nurturing *home*. What new steps can you take to deepen your connection to this concept?

Peace

- From Dying to Live to Living to Die (Ecclesiastes 9:10)
- Retirement and Rediscovery (Numbers 8:23–24)
- Nurturing Peace (Philippians 4:7)

From Dying to Live to Living to Die

ECCLESIASTES 9:10 TELLS US, "WHATEVER YOUR HAND FINDS TO DO, DO it with all your might, for in the realm of the dead, where you are going, there is neither working nor planning nor knowledge nor wisdom." Dying to live and living to die—it's a paradoxical dance we all partake in, isn't it? Ecclesiastes 9:10 nudges us to seize the day, to embrace life with gusto, because, well, we won't be punching the clock in the afterlife!

Let me paint you a picture of my journey, starting from my days as a carefree child, chasing butterflies through fields of dreams and daring to envision a world where anything was possible. Fast-forward to adulthood, and life crashed upon me like a relentless tide—bills to pay, deadlines to meet, and responsibilities mounting with each passing day. In the whirlwind of chaos, I discovered the art of peace, learning to take a step back, breathe deeply, and savor the simple joys that make life truly beautiful.

As the weight of adulthood settled upon my shoulders, I became a maestro of planning, orchestrating every detail with precision and foresight. From meticulously saving every penny for that dream home to charting the course for my family's future, I navigated life's journey with steadfast determination. Yet, amid the hustle and bustle of preparation, the specter of death loomed ever closer, a reminder of life's fragility that many shy away from confronting.

But not me.

With courage as my compass, I delved fearlessly into the conversation surrounding mortality, embracing it with the same passion that fueled my zest for life. I approached the inevitable with a sense of purpose, crafting my exit strategy with the finesse of a seasoned architect. Life insurance policies for my children? Check. Selecting an urn that reflected my essence? Check. And crafting a service program that would evoke laughter and fond memories? Double check!

But my preparations weren't fueled by fear or dread; they were born of a profound understanding that death is not the end but merely a transition to a new chapter in the grand narrative of existence. As I penned the final pages of my life's story, I did so with a heart brimming with anticipation, knowing that the echoes of my adventures would reverberate through the corridors of time, weaving themselves into the tapestry of human experience.

So here's to embracing the paradox of life and death, seizing each moment with boundless passion, planning for the future with unwavering joy, and leaving behind a legacy that transcends the confines of mortality—a legacy of love, laughter, and enduring peace. Cheers to that!

Life Lesson

Embrace the paradox of life and death, seize each moment with passion, plan for the future with joy, and leave behind a legacy of love and laughter.

Retirement and Rediscovery

"The Lord said to Moses, 'This applies to the Levites: Men twenty-five years old or more shall come to take part in the work at the tent of meeting, but at the age of fifty, they must retire from their regular service and work no longer'" (Numbers 8:23–24). Retirement stormed into my life like an unexpected plot twist, transforming uncertainty into a profound journey of rediscovery. No longer confined to clichéd visions of golf courses and Hawaiian shirts, retirement became a catalyst for introspection. Life's curveball prompted a reassessment of my life's narrative, echoing the divine wisdom shared. Reflecting on the Levites' retirement, I recognized the value of embracing change. While standing at the crossroads with my hard hat replaced by a fedora, I am ready to embark on a new adventure—to explore passions, deepen connections, and impart wisdom with newfound peace and purpose.

As I grappled with the loss of my mother, divine guidance emerged, setting the retirement age for Levites and igniting a spark within me. Could this be a celestial pension plan, ordained by the heavens themselves? Suddenly, retirement wasn't merely a choice; it was a calling—a chance to break free from the shackles of the grind and reclaim control over my destiny.

Contemplating this unplanned encore career, I pondered the myriad possibilities. Would I become a beach bum, a world-traveling adventurer, or a connoisseur of exotic teas? With each option, I felt a surge of excitement mingled with trepidation.

Embracing this divine directive, I found solace in stepping away from the rat race, trusting in the unseen hand that guided my path. Though the paycheck might not arrive in the form of a biweekly deposit, I held firm to the belief that divine provision would sustain me through this new chapter.

As I embarked on this uncharted journey, mourning mingled with anticipation, weaving together a tapestry of hope and renewal. This unexpected retirement became my next great adventure—a chance to reinvent, explore, and rediscover life's passions without the relentless ticking of the clock.

The lesson engraved in Numbers 8:23–24 resonated deeply, urging me to embrace the future with courage and faith. With each passing day, I moved forward boldly, trusting in divine guidance to illuminate the path ahead.

So here's to the next chapter—to the uncharted waters of retirement and the boundless possibilities they hold. As I raise my glass to toast this new beginning, I give thanks for the chance to embark on this divine adventure, retirement and all.

Life Lesson

The lesson for me, engraved in Numbers 8:23–24 and etched into the fabric of my newfound retirement, was clear—not to fear the future. Instead, I would move forward boldly, seeking God's guidance and trusting that this next phase of life would bring both peace and exciting possibilities. As I exchanged the hustle and bustle for a slower pace, I thanked God for the chance to embark on this uncharted adventure, retirement and all. Cheers to the next chapter!

Nurturing Peace

Imagine life unfolding like a grand ballroom, where every step and every turn becomes a graceful dance with peace. As Philippians 4:7 reminds us, "And the peace of God, which passeth all understanding, shall keep your hearts and minds through Christ Jesus." In this grand metaphorical ballroom, I find myself not only as the dancer but also the choreographer, moving through life's intricate patterns and unpredictable rhythms.

But let's be real—dancing through life is not always graceful. Sometimes, it's more like stumbling through chaos. That's where the importance of intentional self-care comes in. Peace isn't something that magically arrives; it's cultivated through mindful practices that nourish the body, soul, and spirit.

In this symphony of peace, each act of self-care becomes a vital note in the melody of my well-being. It's not just about the occasional pampering (although a good spa day has its place), but about deeper, meaningful practices that restore balance—like Reiki. Introduced to me later in life, Reiki quickly became a beautiful addition to my self-care and spiritual journey. At first, I saw it as just another wellness practice, but after experiencing its calming energy, I realized how profoundly it complemented everything else in my life. Reiki became more than just therapy; it was a spiritual recalibration, a peaceful pause that allowed me to reconnect with myself on a deeper level.

It's that feeling when all the chaos in your world quiets down, and you can finally breathe again.

Reiki was just one piece of the puzzle. My therapist, my trusted confidant, was another. Like a skilled conductor guiding an orchestra, my therapist helped me navigate the emotional labyrinth of my mind, offering sacred space for reflection and growth. Their wisdom illuminated the path to understanding myself better, showing me how to remove negativity like discordant notes from my life, allowing the seeds of peace to flourish.

Self-care, however, is much more than spiritual practices; it's woven into the very fabric of my daily routine. A healthy lifestyle is my cornerstone. Nourishing food and exercise are not just things to check off a list, but deliberate choices that ground me and keep me resilient. I've learned that by caring for my body, I'm better equipped to handle life's challenges with clarity and positivity.

Music, too, plays a central role in my self-care. Jazz and white noise aren't just background sounds—they're the soundtrack to my serenity. Music shapes my emotional landscape, turning my space into a sanctuary of peace. Words, whether from a favorite book or a meaningful conversation, are my soulful companions. They nourish my mind, reminding me of life's deeper wisdom, helping me stay centered and aligned.

And peace? It's not a solitary endeavor. It's a shared experience, shaped by the people we allow into our lives. The individuals I surround myself with—friends, mentors, family—are not just bystanders but active participants in my symphony of peace. They bring encouragement, positivity, and balance to my life, helping me stay grounded when the world feels unsteady. Their presence helps me maintain that delicate equilibrium between peace and the inevitable chaos that life throws our way.

There's also beauty in my quiet rituals: vision boards, to-do lists, and journaling. These aren't just organizational tools—they are the art of mapping out my dreams and aspirations. They give structure to my thoughts and turn my goals into tangible steps. My home has evolved into more than just a physical space; it's a sanctuary infused with motivation, adorned with words and images that inspire peace and growth.

Even my hobbies, like cycling, have transformed into meditative practices. Each pedal stroke becomes a beat in the rhythm of my thoughts, each turn of the wheel a metaphor for liberation and self-discovery. When I travel, it's not just about seeing new places—it's about feeding my soul with the richness of diverse cultures and perspectives. These experiences are like souvenirs for my spirit, reminders that life's journey is as important as the destination.

Ultimately, peace isn't a destination we reach—it's a continuous journey. It's about cultivating practices and habits that allow serenity to flow into our lives, even in the face of adversity. Whether it's the healing energy of Reiki, the clarity brought by therapy, or the joy found in nurturing relationships, I've discovered that peace isn't about avoiding life's challenges. Rather, it's about embracing them and finding balance through self-care, mindful choices, and intentional living.

So, dear reader, step into your own symphony of peace. My journey is simply one example, but the path to peace is uniquely yours. Life's dance with peace isn't about perfection; it's about crafting a rhythm that resonates with who you are at your core. Through your own rituals, relationships, and practices, may you find the grace to embrace peace—not as a fleeting emotion but as a constant companion guiding you on your journey.

Peace Notes

Join me as I unveil the transformative journey of retirement and rediscovery, guided by the illuminating verses of Numbers 8:23–24. Retirement swept into my life like a gentle breeze, unexpectedly shifting the landscape of my existence and ushering in a profound voyage of self-discovery. Freed from the constraints of conventional norms, I found myself at a crossroads, embracing change with a newfound sense of purpose.

No longer confined by the rigidity of routine, I embarked on an odyssey of introspection, reevaluating the narrative of my life and embracing the unknown with open arms. Trading in my hard hat for a fedora symbolized more than just a change in attire—it represented a shift toward embracing new opportunities, nurturing meaningful relationships, and navigating life's journey with tranquility, all while anchored by an unwavering faith in God.

As I delve deeper into the art of nurturing peace, drawing inspiration from Philippians 4:7, I invite you to join me in exploring the profound wisdom encapsulated in the dance of peace. Life unfolds before us like a grand ballroom, where moments of serene contemplation interlace seamlessly with storms of adversity. Through my own experiences, I extend an invitation for you to discover the rhythm that resonates within your soul.

May your journey be adorned with intentional movements, crafting a symphony of life that harmonizes with your essence. As you navigate the intricate steps of existence, may you find solace in the melodies of peace, each note adding to the masterpiece of your being.

Workbook Section

Deep Reflections

- Prompt: Reflecting on the transition to a slower pace and embracing retirement as an uncharted adventure, how do you find peace in trusting the future and seeking divine guidance, as illuminated by Numbers 8:23–24? Considering the symphony of practices that resonate with your soul, how do you craft intentional movements that harmonize with the essence of your being, creating a masterpiece of peace in each step? Moreover, how do you perceive the profound beauty in life's dance with peace, recognizing that it's not just about the destination but the journey itself?

Actionable Steps

1. Finding Peace in Trusting the Future
   - Reflect: Consider how the transition to a slower pace or retirement is a new adventure. How do you find peace in trusting that this phase of life holds opportunities for growth and divine guidance?
   - Write: Describe your feelings about this transition. How do you seek divine guidance, and how does Numbers 8:23–24 inspire you to trust the future?

2. Journaling Exercise
   - Explore: Write about the practices and rituals that resonate with your soul and contribute to your sense of peace. How do these practices help you create harmony and balance in your life?
   - Contemplate: Reflect on how you can integrate these practices into your daily routine to enhance your sense of inner peace.

3. Crafting Intentional Movements
    -   Identify: Identify specific actions or changes you can make to align with your essence and create peace in your life. What intentional movements can you adopt to harmonize with your inner self?
    -   Act: Develop a plan for implementing these intentional movements. How can you incorporate them into your daily life to create a masterpiece of peace?

4. Perceiving the Beauty in Life's Dance with Peace
    -   Reflect: Contemplate the concept of peace as a dance rather than a destination. How do you experience the beauty in the journey of finding peace, rather than focusing solely on the end goal?
    -   Document: Write about moments in your life when you have felt at peace. How does this understanding of peace as a dance influence your perspective and approach to life's journey?

5. Embracing the Journey
    -   Explore: Reflect on how embracing the journey, with its ups and downs, contributes to a deeper sense of peace. How can you appreciate the process and the growth that comes with each step of your journey?
    -   Illustrate: Create a visual or written representation of your journey toward peace. How does this imagery help you see the beauty in the process?

6. Daily Affirmation
    -   Write: Craft an affirmation that reflects your commitment to finding and nurturing peace through trust, intentionality, and appreciation of the journey, such as "I embrace the journey of life with peace, trusting in divine guidance and crafting intentional movements that harmonize with my essence."

- Repeat: Recite this affirmation daily to reinforce your dedication to finding and creating peace in your life.

7. 7. Reflection on Progress

   - Monitor: At the end of each week, review how your sense of peace has evolved. How has your approach to embracing the journey and trusting the future influenced your overall peace of mind?
   - Adjust: Consider any adjustments needed in your practices or perspective. What new steps can you take to further enhance your sense of peace?

Epilogue

- A Journey to Strength, Growth, and the Unwavering Spirit

A Journey to Strength, Growth, and the Unwavering Spirit

In the closing of this narrative, we are reminded that life is indeed a journey—a journey to strength, growth, and unwavering spirit. As we step into the embroidery of my life, woven with threads of divine guidance and resilience, we witness the triumph over life's relentless storms.

This is more than just a memoir; it is a symphony of resilience, a testament to the transformative power of living in communion with God. As we journey together through these pages, may the echoes of my experiences resonate in the corridors of your soul, inspiring reflection and recognition of the beauty that emerges even from life's darkest corners.

Among the narratives I've recounted, some have been wrought with challenges and pain. Yet, through introspection and resilience, I've endeavored to present them to you with the hope that they may serve as beacons of guidance and sources of reassurance for the journeys that lie ahead.

While there are many more tales within the folds of my family's history, it is my sincere hope that amid these shared stories, you find solace, courage, and moments of joy to persevere and revel in life's triumphs.

As I continue to navigate the chapters of my life, there remain stories awaiting resolution, narratives yet to be unearthed and shared. It is my aspiration that one day, I may summon the strength to bring these narratives to light and share them with you, my cherished readers. Until that moment arrives, take comfort in the unwavering presence of faith, knowing that amid life's uncertainties, we are accompanied by the divine presence of God.

But as this book comes to a close, I am honored to share the words of my daughter, Meiya Carter, whose wisdom beautifully encapsulates the essence of our shared journey. She reminds us that life's lessons are universal, regardless of their origin, and that true wisdom lies in the ability to extract meaning from them.

As I bid farewell to this saga, standing amid the heartbeat of Newark, I stand not only as Shana Burnett but as a testament to the indomitable spirit that emerges from adversity. Born into the embrace of concrete streets, shaped by struggle and strength, I've worn many hats—but beyond titles and accolades, my journey unfolds as a resilient dance through shadows, a divine waltz with life's intricacies.

In the grand theater of existence, I found solace in the shadows, a serene beach amid tumultuous waves. The silent conversations with God, the unanswered pleas, became the backdrop of transformation. The shadows, once adversaries, became sculptors of strength, revealing the unyielding core within.

As I navigated the labyrinth of my past, scars transformed into testaments of triumph. The theater of my life, unfairly cast and marred, became a canvas where resilience painted vibrant strokes over pain's stains. The cloak of ugliness became a tapestry, weaving adversity into triumph.

The journey was not without despair and questioning, but I learned that divine assurance manifests as strength to endure unanswered questions and courage to keep knocking on doors when they seem bolted.

Adversity transformed into a bridge, leading to the discovery of inner strength. God's promise guided me not as a shield from hardship but as a companion through the storm. I stand not as a victim but as a survivor, a testament to the potential for growth, healing, and discovering inner light within shadows.

As the curtain falls, let it rise in the hearts of those who journeyed with me. Let the symphony of shadows and strength inspire others to dance through challenges, finding resilience in adversity's face. Even in life's darkest corners, the potential for growth and unyielding strength await, unveiled in life's divine dance. Embrace your journey with grace!

Unveiling Grace

A Journey Through Life
and a Walk with God

WORKBOOK

Chapter on Faith

Deep Reflections

- Prompt: As you journey through life's intricate pathways, do you rely on faith to guide you through unexplored territories, or do you find comfort in sticking to familiar routes? When faced with uncertainty and doubt, do you seek solace in divine wisdom, or are you tempted by quick fixes and easy solutions? In the midst of life's storms, do you tap into the inner strength provided by your faith, or do you struggle under the weight of adversity? Where do you currently find yourself on your spiritual journey?

Scriptural Foundations

- A Journey of Faith, Laughter, and Spiritual Awakening (Isaiah 40:8): "The grass withers and the flowers fall, but the word of our God endures forever." Reflect on how this scripture underscores the enduring nature of God's Word as a constant guide through your spiritual journey, providing faith and renewal amid the changing seasons of life.
- Guided through the Wilderness (Proverbs 3:5-6): "Trust in the Lord with all your heart and lean not on your own understanding; in all your ways submit to him, and he will make your paths straight." Consider how this scripture encourages you to rely on

divine guidance and trust in God's plan, especially when navigating uncertain or challenging times.

- Taming the Storm Within (Exodus 15:2): "The Lord is my strength and my defense; he has become my salvation. He is my God, and I will praise him, my father's God, and I will exalt him." Reflect on how this scripture portrays the Lord as a source of strength and salvation, helping you find inner peace and stability during life's turbulent moments.

Actionable Steps

1. Self-Assessment

- Reflect: Write down your current understanding and practice of faith. What role does faith play in your daily life? Are you more inclined to trust in divine guidance, or do you lean on familiar, safe choices?

_____

_____

_____

_____

_____

- Evaluate: Think about recent challenges you've faced. Did you turn to your faith for strength and guidance? If not, what alternative paths did you take?

_____

_____

_____

_____

_____

_____

2. Journaling Exercise

- Explore: Describe a time when you were at a crossroads in life. How did faith influence your decision? What was the outcome, and how did it shape your spiritual journey?

_____

_____

_____

_____

_____

- Contemplate: Consider moments of doubt or uncertainty. What has prevented you from fully trusting in your faith? How can you overcome these barriers?

_____

_____

_____

_____

_____

3. Faith in Action

- Commit: Identify one area of your life where you can actively practice your faith. This could be through prayer, meditation, or stepping out in faith in a situation that feels uncertain.

_____

_____

_____

_____

_____

- Act: Take a small but meaningful step this week that requires you to trust in divine guidance rather than relying solely on your own understanding.

_____

_____

_____

_____

_____

4. Guided Prayer or Meditation

- Focus: Spend time each day in prayer or meditation, asking for the strength to lean into your faith during life's challenges.

_____

_____

_____

_____

_____

- Visualize: Imagine yourself walking through a difficult situation with faith as your guide. How does this change your perspective and approach?

_____

_____

_____

_____

_____

5. Daily Affirmation

- Write: Create an affirmation centered on faith, such as "I trust in the divine plan for my life and walk in faith, knowing that I am guided and supported."

_____

_____

_____

_____

_____

- Repeat: Begin each day by reciting this affirmation, grounding yourself in faith as you navigate your journey.

_____

_____

_____

_____

_____

6. Reflection on Progress

- Monitor: At the end of each week, reflect on how your faith has influenced your actions and decisions. What changes have you noticed in your mindset and approach to challenges?

_____

_____

_____

_____

_____

- Adjust: If you find areas where faith has been difficult to apply, consider what might be holding you back and how you can deepen your trust.

_____

_____

_____

_____

_____

Chapter on Identity

Deep Reflections

- Prompt: Reflecting on life's chaos and diversity, how do you define your identity? What facets of your background, experiences, and values contribute to shaping who you are? Amid life's tempests, do you envision yourself as a dancer, gracefully navigating challenges with resilience as your VIP pass? How does your capacity to rebound from adversity shape your understanding of self?

Scriptural Foundations

- From Stone to Flesh (Ezekiel 36:26): "I will give you a new heart and put a new spirit in you; I will remove from you your heart of stone and give you a heart of flesh." Reflect on how this scripture represents the transformation of your identity, emphasizing the renewal and softening of your inner being as you embrace a new, more authentic self.
- The Power of a Simple Word (Psalm 119:105): "Your word is a lamp to my feet and a light for my path." Contemplate how this scripture highlights the role of divine guidance in shaping your identity, providing clarity and direction as you navigate your journey.
- Embracing Unity in the Face of Colorism and Racism (Galatians 3:28): "There is neither Jew nor Gentile, neither slave nor free, neither male nor female, for you are all one in Christ Jesus." Reflect on how this scripture calls for unity and equality, encouraging you to embrace and celebrate your identity within the context of a diverse and inclusive community.

Actionable Steps

1. Self-Exploration

- Reflect: Write about the core elements that define your identity. Consider your cultural background, family traditions, personal experiences, and deeply held values.

_____

_____

_____

_____

_____

_____

_____

_____

_____

_____

- Analyze: How do these aspects of your identity influence the way you view yourself and interact with the world around you?

_____

_____

_____

_____

_____

_____

_____

_____

_____

2. Journaling Exercise

- Explore: Describe a situation where you faced significant challenges or adversity. How did your identity help you navigate through this period? Did it empower you, or were there aspects you needed to reconcile?

_____

_____

_____

_____

_____

- Contemplate: Think about a time when you had to adapt or change aspects of your identity. How did this experience affect your sense of self?

_____

_____

_____

_____

_____

3. Visualizing Resilience

- Envision: Picture yourself as a dancer moving through life's challenges. How does this imagery resonate with you? What qualities do you possess that allow you to move gracefully through adversity?

_____

_____

_____

_____

- Illustrate: Create a visual representation (a drawing, collage, or digital art) that symbolizes your identity and resilience. Reflect on how this process deepens your understanding of yourself.

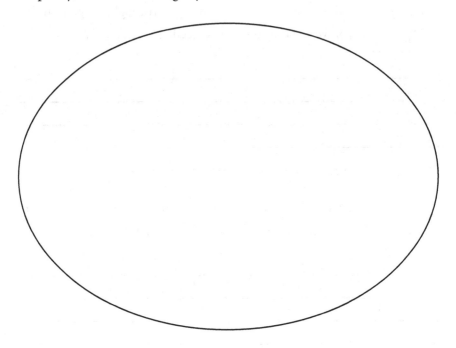

4. Resilience in Action

- Identify: Choose one area in your life where you currently face challenges. How can your understanding of your identity and resilience help you approach this situation differently?

_____

_____

_____

_____

_____

- Act: Implement a small but significant action that reflects your identity and demonstrates your resilience. This could be standing firm in your values, embracing a new challenge, or supporting someone else in their journey.

_____

_____

_____

_____

_____

5. Daily Affirmation

- Write: Craft an affirmation that reinforces your sense of identity and resilience, such as "I am grounded in my true self and navigate life's challenges with grace and strength."

_____

_____

_____

_____

_____

- Repeat: Recite this affirmation daily, letting it remind you of your inherent resilience and the power of your identity.

_____

_____

_____

_____

_____

6. Reflection on Growth

- Review: At the end of each week, reflect on how your understanding of your identity has evolved. How has your resilience been tested and strengthened?

_____

_____

_____

_____

_____

- Adjust: Consider any areas where you might need to further align your actions with your identity. What steps can you take to ensure that your identity continues to guide you through life's challenges?

_____

_____

_____

_____

_____

Chapter on Solitude

Deep Reflections

- Prompt: Amid life's grand tapestry, where do you find solace in solitude? Reflecting on the echoes of resilience within profound silence, do you see it as the backdrop to a divine symphony waiting to unfold? As you journey through the seasons of love, reflection, challenges, and renewal, how do you navigate the dance of relationships with consistency as your choreography and God as your partner? Moreover, in embracing imperfection and navigating unexpected plot twists, how does divine love guide you through the labyrinth of life's challenges?

Scriptural Foundations

- In the Depths of Desolation (1 Corinthians 16:13–14): "Be on your guard; stand firm in the faith; be courageous; be strong. Do everything in love." Reflect on how this scripture encourages steadfastness and strength in times of solitude, emphasizing the importance of faith, courage, and love even when facing challenges alone.
- Seasons of the Heart (Jeremiah 29:11–13): "'For I know the plans I have for you,' declares the Lord, 'plans to prosper you and not to harm you, plans to give you a hope and a future. Then you will call on me and come and pray to me, and I will listen to you. You will seek me and find me when you seek me with all your heart.'" Contemplate how this scripture reassures you of God's plans and presence, guiding you through the seasons of solitude with hope and divine promise.
- God's Transformative Love (Psalm 143): "Hear my prayer, Lord; listen to my cry for mercy. In your faithfulness and righteousness come to my relief. Do not bring your servant into judgment, for

151

no one living is righteous before you. The enemy pursues me, he crushes me to the ground; he makes me dwell in the darkness like those long dead. So my spirit grows faint within me; my heart within me is dismayed. I remember the days of long ago; I meditate on all your works and consider what your hands have done. I spread out my hands to you; I thirst for you like a parched land." Reflect on how this scripture speaks to the deep cry for relief and connection in solitude and how God's transformative love provides solace and renewal during times of deep personal reflection.

Actionable Steps

1. Embracing Solitude

- Reflect: Spend time in solitude and reflect on where you find peace in being alone. How does solitude allow you to connect with your inner self and divine guidance?

_____

_____

_____

_____

_____

- Write: Describe moments when solitude has provided clarity or comfort in your life. How does it serve as a foundation for your resilience?

_____

_____

_____

_____

_____

2. Journaling Exercise

- Explore: Write about a time when silence and solitude played a crucial role in your spiritual or personal growth. How did these moments shape your understanding of yourself and your relationship with God?

_____

_____

_____

_____

_____

- Contemplate: Consider the role of solitude in your daily life. How can you intentionally create space for it, allowing it to become a regular practice?

_____

_____

_____

_____

_____

3. Divine Symphony Visualization

- Envision: Imagine the silence of solitude as the backdrop to a divine symphony. What melodies or harmonies do you hear when you quiet your mind and listen deeply?

_____

_____

_____

_____

_____

- Illustrate: Create a piece of art or a written reflection that symbolizes this divine symphony. How does this visualization deepen your connection to divine love and guidance?

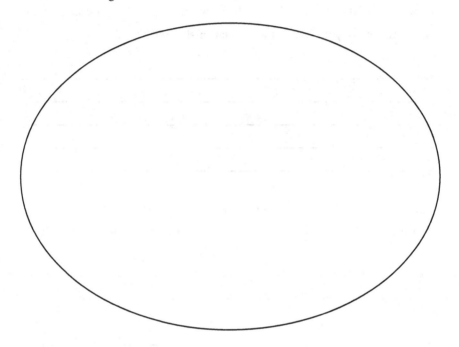

4. Navigating Relationships

- Identify: Reflect on your relationships and how you navigate them with consistency and faith. How does your relationship with God influence the way you engage with others?

_____

_____

_____

_____

_____

- Act: Choose one relationship where you can apply more intentionality, using solitude to reflect on how you can show up more consistently and lovingly.

_____

_____

_____

_____

_____

5. Embracing Imperfection

- Accept: Acknowledge the imperfections in your life and relationships. How does embracing these imperfections allow you to grow and learn?

_____

_____

_____

_____

_____

- Act: Identify one area where you can let go of perfectionism and allow divine love to guide you through unexpected challenges. What small steps can you take to trust in this guidance?

_____

_____

_____

_____

_____

6. Daily Affirmation

- Write: Create an affirmation centered on solitude, divine love, and resilience, such as "In the silence of solitude, I find divine love guiding me through every challenge with grace and strength."

_____

_____

_____

_____

_____

- Repeat: Begin each day with this affirmation, grounding yourself in the peace that solitude and divine guidance provide.

_____

_____

_____

_____

_____

7. Reflection on Journey

- Monitor: At the end of each week, reflect on how solitude has influenced your spiritual journey and relationships. What insights have you gained from embracing quiet moments and divine guidance?

_____

_____

_____

_____

_____

- Adjust: Consider any areas where you might need to deepen your practice of solitude or trust in divine love. What steps can you take to continue navigating life's challenges with resilience and faith?

_____

_____

_____

_____

_____

Chapter on Transformation

Deep Reflections

- Prompt: Reflecting on the profound lesson of inner beauty and the transformative power of words, how do you perceive your role as the lead character in the grand play of life? How do you actively cultivate authenticity in your journey of faith and self-discovery amid life's challenges and societal pressures? As you navigate the narratives you weave and the relationships you cultivate, how do you harness the wisdom gained through the dance of words and understanding to shape your story with purpose? Moreover, how do you allow the echoes of your inner truths and the guiding light of grace to orchestrate your transformation journey in the symphony of existence?

Scriptural Foundations

- The Transformative Mirror (Romans 12:2): "Do not conform to the pattern of this world, but be transformed by the renewing of your mind. Then you will be able to test and approve what God's will is—his good, pleasing and perfect will." Reflect on how this scripture emphasizes the process of transformation through the renewal of your mind, guiding you to align with God's will and achieve true personal change.
- A First Lady's Journey through Church Circles and Self-Discovery (1 Timothy 3:1–7): "Here is a trustworthy saying: Whoever aspires to be an overseer desires a noble task. Now the overseer is to be above reproach, faithful to his wife, temperate, self-controlled, respectable, hospitable, able to teach, not given to drunkenness, not violent but gentle, not quarrelsome, not a lover of money. He must manage his own family well and see that his children obey him with proper respect. (If anyone does not know how to manage

his own family, how can he take care of God's church?) He must not be a recent convert, or he may become conceited and fall under the same judgment as the devil. He must also have a good reputation with outsiders, so that he will not fall into disgrace and into the devil's trap." Consider how this scripture provides guidance on leadership and personal growth, highlighting the qualities needed for transformation and effective leadership within a faith community.

- Harmony in the Therapeutic Symphony (Isaiah 55:11): "So is my word that goes out from my mouth: It will not return to me empty, but will accomplish what I desire and achieve the purpose for which I sent it." Reflect on how this scripture illustrates the powerful and purposeful nature of God's Word in bringing about transformation, ensuring that divine promises and intentions are fulfilled.

Actionable Steps

1. Embracing Inner Beauty

- Reflect: Spend time contemplating what inner beauty means to you. How do your actions, thoughts, and words reflect this inner beauty? How does it shape your interactions with others?

_____

_____

_____

_____

_____

_____

_____

- Write: Describe moments in your life when you felt truly beautiful from the inside out. How did these moments influence your journey of self-discovery and faith?

_____

_____

_____

_____

_____

2. Journaling Exercise

- Explore: Reflect on your role as the lead character in your life. How have you embraced this role, and in what ways do you sometimes shy away from it? What steps can you take to fully embody this role with authenticity?

_____

_____

_____

_____

_____

_____

- Contemplate: Write about the narratives you've created in your life. How do these narratives align with your true self and your journey of transformation?

_____

_____

_____

_____

3. Cultivating Authenticity

- Identify: Think about areas in your life where you feel pressure to conform to societal expectations. How can you practice authenticity in these areas, staying true to your values and beliefs?

_____

_____

_____

_____

_____

- Act: Choose one situation this week where you will consciously practice authenticity, even if it feels challenging. Reflect on the outcome and how it affects your sense of self.

_____

_____

_____

_____

_____

4. Harnessing Wisdom

- Envision: Picture the words and wisdom you've gained throughout your life as a dance that shapes your narrative. How can you use this wisdom to guide your decisions and interactions?

_____

_____

_____

_____

- Illustrate: Create a visual or written representation of how the transformative power of words has shaped your life. How does this representation inspire you to continue growing and evolving?

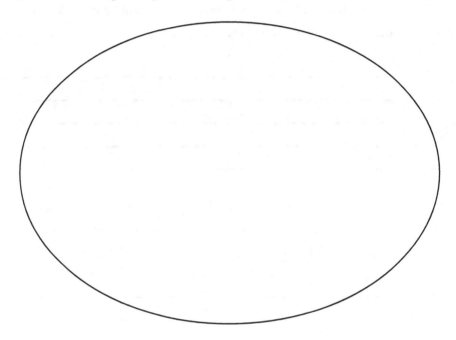

5. Guided Meditation

- Focus: Spend time in meditation, allowing the echoes of your inner truths and the light of grace to guide your thoughts. How do these elements support your transformation journey?

_____

_____

_____

_____

_____

- Visualize: Imagine your life as a symphony, with each experience adding to the harmony of your existence. How does this imagery help you embrace your journey with grace and purpose?

_____

_____

_____

_____

_____

6. Daily Affirmation

- Write: Create an affirmation that reflects your commitment to authenticity, inner beauty, and transformation, such as "I embrace my journey with authenticity and grace, allowing the wisdom of my inner truths to guide me."

_____

_____

_____

_____

_____

- Repeat: Start each day by reciting this affirmation, grounding yourself in the transformative power of your words and actions.

_____

_____

_____

_____

_____

7. Reflection on Progress

- Monitor: At the end of each week, reflect on how you've embraced your role as the lead character in your life's story. How has your understanding of inner beauty and authenticity evolved?

_____

_____

_____

_____

_____

- Adjust: Consider any areas where you may need to further align your actions with your inner truths. What steps can you take to continue your journey of transformation with purpose and grace?

_____

_____

_____

_____

_____

Chapter on Purpose

Deep Reflections

- Prompt: Reflecting on the lessons learned amid life's storms and shadows, how do you perceive your journey toward discovering purpose? As you navigate challenges and embrace the transformative love surrounding you, how do you view stumbling blocks—as obstacles or stepping stones toward a brighter future? Moreover, how does unwavering faith guide you through the crucible of difficulties, shaping you into a resilient being capable of weathering any storm? In contemplating these lessons, how do you envision your path forward, illuminated by the radiant light that awaits beyond the clouds and driven by the purpose that arises from overcoming adversity?

Scriptural Foundations

- Illuminating the Darkness with God's Beauty (Romans 8:28): "And we know that in all things God works for the good of those who love him, who have been called according to his purpose." Reflect on how this scripture assures that even in challenging times, God's purpose and goodness are at work, guiding you toward a greater understanding of your purpose.
- Rediscovering the Lost Pieces Within (Proverbs 16:3): "Commit to the Lord whatever you do, and he will establish your plans." Contemplate how this scripture encourages you to align your actions with divine guidance, helping you rediscover and fulfill your purpose through committed and purposeful living.
- Storms as Stepping Stones (James 1:12–14): "Blessed is the one who perseveres under trial because, having stood the test, that person will receive the crown of life that the Lord has promised

to those who love him. When tempted, no one should say, 'God is tempting me.' For God cannot be tempted by evil, nor does he tempt anyone; but each person is tempted when they are dragged away by their own evil desire and enticed." Reflect on how this scripture highlights the value of enduring trials and temptations, viewing them as opportunities for growth and stepping stones toward fulfilling your divine purpose.

Actionable Steps

1. Understanding Purpose

- Reflect: Think about significant challenges you have faced and the lessons you have learned from them. How have these experiences shaped your understanding of your life's purpose?

_____

_____

_____

_____

_____

- Write: Describe a moment when you discovered a new aspect of your purpose through adversity. How did this revelation affect your journey and outlook?

_____

_____

_____

_____

_____

2. Journaling Exercise

- Explore: Write about a recent stumbling block or difficulty you faced. How did you perceive it—as an obstacle or a stepping stone? What did you learn from this experience?

_____

_____

_____

_____

_____

- Contemplate: Reflect on how you can shift your perspective on challenges to view them as opportunities for growth. How can this change in perspective help you move forward?

_____

_____

_____

_____

_____

3. Navigating Challenges

- Identify: Identify a current challenge or difficulty you are facing. How can you use your unwavering faith to guide you through this situation?

_____

_____

_____

_____

_____

- Act: Develop a plan for how you will approach this challenge with faith and resilience. What steps can you take to stay grounded and focused on your purpose?

_____

_____

_____

_____

_____

_____

_____

_____

4. Harnessing Transformative Love

- Envision: Visualize the transformative love surrounding you as a guiding force in your journey. How does this love help you navigate through the storms and shadows of life?

_____

_____

_____

_____

_____

_____

_____

_____

- Illustrate: Create a visual representation or a written reflection that captures the essence of this transformative love and its role in your journey toward purpose.

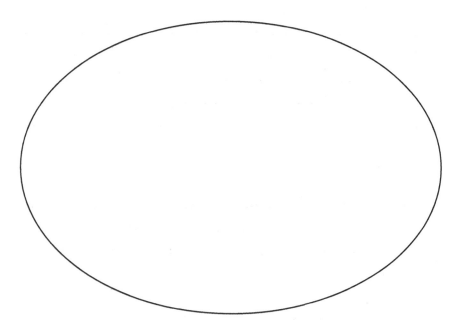

5. Path Forward

- Reflect: Consider how your path forward is illuminated by the lessons learned and the light that awaits beyond your current challenges. How does this vision shape your goals and actions?

_____

_____

_____

_____

_____

- Plan: Outline a plan for how you will move forward, driven by the purpose that arises from overcoming adversity. What specific actions will you take to align with this purpose?

_____

_____

_____

_____

_____

6. Daily Affirmation

- Write: Craft an affirmation that encapsulates your commitment to discovering and living out your purpose, such as "I embrace life's challenges as opportunities for growth, guided by unwavering faith and illuminated by the light of purpose."

_____

_____

_____

_____

_____

- Repeat: Recite this affirmation daily to reinforce your focus on purpose and resilience.

_____

_____

_____

_____

_____

7.   Reflection on Progress

- Monitor: At the end of each week, review how your perspective on purpose and challenges has evolved. How has your faith guided you through difficulties?

_____

_____

_____

_____

_____

- Adjust: Consider any adjustments you need to make in your approach to challenges or in your pursuit of purpose. What steps can you take to continue moving forward with clarity and conviction?

_____

_____

_____

_____

_____

Chapter on Freedom

Deep Reflections

- Prompt: Reflecting on the profound lesson of embracing love in its purest form, how do you perceive the concept of freedom within the intricately woven tapestry of life? As you navigate the threads of kindness, understanding, and love, how do you find liberation in recognizing and appreciating the divine beauty within yourself and others? Moreover, in acknowledging life's miracles and blessings, how does this awareness elevate your existence beyond the confines of your own story, opening the door to a more profound sense of freedom and connection?

Scriptural Foundations

- A Journey from Stifled to Empowered (Colossians 3:21): "Fathers, do not embitter your children, or they will become discouraged." Reflect on how this scripture emphasizes the importance of fostering an environment of encouragement and empowerment, promoting freedom from discouragement and negative influences.
- Blossom of Resilience (Ezekiel 7:10): "The day is here! The doom has come! The rod has budded, arrogance has blossomed!" Contemplate how this scripture illustrates the emergence of resilience and the growth that comes from overcoming adversity, even in challenging times.
- Unveiling the Miracles (1 John 4:8): "Whoever does not love does not know God, because God is love." Reflect on how this scripture reveals the essence of divine love as a foundation for true freedom, understanding that embracing love leads to a deeper experience of freedom and connection.

Actionable Steps

1. Exploring the Concept of Freedom

- Reflect: Contemplate what freedom means to you within the broader context of life's tapestry. How do love, kindness, and understanding play a role in your sense of freedom?

_____

_____

_____

_____

- Write: Describe a moment when you experienced a profound sense of freedom through acts of love and kindness. How did this experience shift your perspective on freedom?

_____

_____

_____

_____

2. Journaling Exercise

- Explore: Write about how recognizing and appreciating the divine beauty in yourself and others has affected your sense of liberation. How has this appreciation influenced your relationships and self-view?

_____

_____

_____

_____

_____

- Contemplate: Reflect on how acknowledging life's miracles and blessings has elevated your experience beyond your own story. How does this broader awareness contribute to a deeper sense of freedom?

_____

_____

_____

_____

_____

3. Navigating the Threads of Life

- Identify: Identify a specific area in your life where you feel constrained. How can kindness, understanding, and love help you navigate and transform this constraint into a space of freedom?

_____

_____

_____

_____

_____

- Act: Develop a plan to incorporate more acts of kindness and understanding in this area. How can these actions help you feel more liberated and connected?

_____

_____

_____

_____

_____

4. Embracing Divine Beauty

- Visualize: Picture yourself and others enveloped in a divine light that highlights your inherent beauty. How does this visualization affect your sense of freedom and self-worth?

_____

_____

_____

_____

_____

- Illustrate: Create a visual representation or written reflection that captures the divine beauty you see in yourself and others. How does this perspective enhance your feelings of freedom and connection?

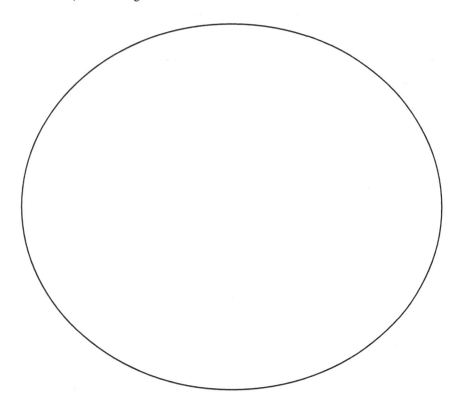

5. Acknowledging Miracles and Blessings

- Reflect: Take time to recognize and appreciate the miracles and blessings in your life. How does this awareness shift your focus from limitations to a broader sense of freedom?

_____

_____

_____

_____

- Document: Keep a gratitude journal where you record daily miracles and blessings. Reflect on how this practice contributes to a more profound sense of freedom and connection.

_____

_____

_____

_____

_____

6. Daily Affirmation

- Write: Craft an affirmation that reflects your commitment to embracing love and recognizing divine beauty, such as "I embrace the freedom that comes from recognizing the divine beauty in myself and others, allowing love to guide my journey."

_____

_____

_____

_____

_____

- Repeat: Start each day by reciting this affirmation, reinforcing your commitment to freedom and connection through love and appreciation.

_____

_____

_____

_____

_____

7. Reflection on Progress

- Monitor: At the end of each week, review how your understanding of freedom has evolved. How has embracing love and kindness influenced your sense of liberation?

_____

_____

_____

_____

_____

- Adjust: Consider any adjustments needed in your approach to experiencing freedom and connection. What new steps can you take to deepen this understanding and practice?

_____

_____

_____

_____

_____

Chapter on Gifts

Deep Reflections

- Prompt: Reflecting on the symphony of life and the concept of gifts bestowed upon us, how do you perceive the role of nurturing and celebrating these divine blessings? As you navigate the grand stage of existence, how do you harmonize the unique melodies of your gifts with the ongoing symphony of life? Moreover, in embracing and celebrating your gifts, how do you contribute to the collective harmony of existence, ensuring that your melody resonates through the gifts God has bestowed upon you?

Scriptural Foundations

- A Tale of Generosity, Traditions, and Joyful Giving (Matthew 2:10–11): "When they saw the star, they were overjoyed. On coming to the house, they saw the child with his mother Mary, and they bowed down and worshiped him. Then they opened their treasures and presented him with gifts of gold, frankincense, and myrrh." Reflect on how this scripture highlights the beauty of generous giving and the joy of sharing blessings, drawing inspiration from the wise men's act of honoring Jesus with their gifts.

- Celebrating Children as Life's Melodic Treasures (Psalm 127:3): "Children are a heritage from the Lord, offspring a reward from him." Contemplate how this scripture underscores the preciousness of children as gifts from God and the importance of cherishing and nurturing them as integral parts of life's journey.

Actionable Steps

1. Understanding Your Gifts

- Reflect: Contemplate the gifts and talents you believe have been bestowed upon you. How do these gifts contribute to your sense of purpose and fulfillment in life?

_____

_____

_____

_____

_____

- Write: Describe specific moments when you felt your gifts were particularly influential. How did nurturing and celebrating these gifts affect your experience?

_____

_____

_____

_____

_____

2. Journaling Exercise

- Explore: Write about how you currently nurture and celebrate your gifts. How does this process help you maintain a sense of connection and harmony in your life?

_____

_____

_____

_____

_____

- Contemplate: Reflect on ways you can further enhance your ability to harmonize your gifts with the ongoing symphony of life. What new practices can you implement?

_____

_____

_____

_____

_____

3. Harmonizing Your Gifts

- Identify: Identify areas in your life where your gifts could be better integrated or expressed. How can you align these gifts with the broader context of your life's purpose?

_____

_____

_____

_____

_____

- Act: Develop a plan for how you will bring your gifts into these areas, ensuring they contribute positively to your personal and collective harmony.

_____

_____

_____

_____

4. Celebrating Divine Blessings

- Visualize: Imagine your gifts as unique melodies within the grand symphony of existence. How does this visualization affect your understanding of their role and significance?

_____

_____

_____

_____

_____

_____

- Illustrate: Create a visual representation or written reflection on how celebrating your gifts enhances your life and contributes to the collective harmony. How does this celebration influence your interactions with others?

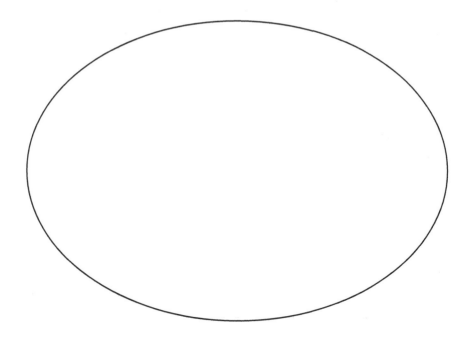

5. Contributing to Collective Harmony

- Reflect: Consider how your gifts contribute to the collective harmony of existence. How do your actions and contributions resonate with the broader community or world?

_____

_____

_____

_____

_____

- Document: Write about ways you actively ensure your gifts are used for the greater good. What steps can you take to enhance this contribution?

_____

_____

_____

_____

_____

6. Daily Affirmation

- Write: Craft an affirmation that reflects your commitment to nurturing and celebrating your gifts, such as "I honor and celebrate the divine gifts bestowed upon me, harmonizing my unique melodies with the symphony of life."

_____

_____

_____

_____

_____

- Repeat: Recite this affirmation daily to reinforce your dedication to embracing and contributing your gifts.

_____

_____

_____

_____

_____

7. 7. Reflection on Progress

- Monitor: At the end of each week, review how your understanding and celebration of your gifts have evolved. How has this process affected your sense of purpose and connection?

_____

_____

_____

_____

_____

- Adjust: Consider any adjustments needed to better integrate and celebrate your gifts. What new steps can you take to ensure your gifts contribute to the collective harmony?

_____

_____

_____

_____

_____

Chapter on Love

Deep Reflections

- Prompt: Considering the profound lesson of agape love illuminated by Matthew 5:44 and exemplified by the resilience of your mother or father, how do you navigate the complexities of love amid life's two-timing tales and unexpected twists? Reflecting on your experiences, how do you discern between genuine love and deceit, safeguarding your heart while embracing the enduring power of love to persist through laughter, tears, and absurdities? Moreover, how does your understanding of agape love shape your relationships with fellow believers or perceived enemies and guide you toward greater compassion and understanding?

Scriptural Foundations

- Love, Laughter, and Two-Timing Tomfoolery (Matthew 5:44): "But I tell you, love your enemies and pray for those who persecute you." Reflect on how this scripture challenges us to embody unconditional love, even in difficult situations, and how it guides us to maintain compassion and understanding despite adversities.
- The Compass of Love (1 Corinthians 16:14): "Do everything in love." Consider how this scripture serves as a guiding principle in all interactions, encouraging you to infuse every action with genuine love and kindness, thereby shaping your relationships and daily life.

Actionable Steps

1. Understanding Agape Love

- Reflect: Contemplate the concept of agape love as described in Matthew 5:44. How do you understand this form of unconditional, selfless love? How does it compare to other forms of love you've experienced?

_____

_____

_____

_____

_____

_____

- Write: Describe how the resilience of your mother or father exemplifies agape love. How has their example influenced your view on navigating love amid complexities?

_____

_____

_____

_____

_____

_____

2. Journaling Exercise

- Explore: Write about a time when you had to navigate the complexities of love amid challenges. How did you discern between genuine love and deceit in this situation?

_____

_____

_____

_____

_____

- Contemplate: Reflect on how you protected your heart while maintaining a capacity to love. What strategies did you employ to ensure you embraced love's enduring power?

_____

_____

_____

_____

_____

3. Navigating Love's Complexities

- Identify: Identify a recent situation where you encountered two-timing tales or unexpected twists in a relationship. How did you handle these complexities while striving to remain true to agape love?

_____

_____

_____

_____

_____

- Act: Develop a plan for how you will approach similar situations in the future. What steps can you take to safeguard your heart while embracing the resilience and enduring power of love?

_____

_____

_____

_____

_____

4.   Discerning Genuine Love

- Reflect: Reflect on your experiences of discernment in relationships. How have you learned to distinguish between genuine love and deceit?

_____

_____

_____

_____

_____

- Document: Write about how you have safeguarded your heart while maintaining the ability to embrace love through life's ups and downs. What insights have you gained from these experiences?

_____

_____

_____

_____

_____

5. Shaping Relationships with Compassion

- Explore: Consider how your understanding of agape love influences your relationships with fellow believers and perceived enemies. How does this perspective guide you toward greater compassion and understanding?

_____

_____

_____

_____

_____

_____

_____

- Illustrate: Create a visual or written representation of how agape love shapes your interactions and relationships. How does this influence your approach to others, especially those with whom you have conflicts?

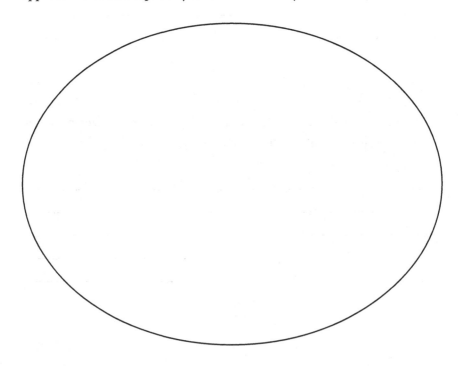

6. Daily Affirmation

- Write: Craft an affirmation that reflects your commitment to embracing agape love and navigating relationship complexities with compassion, such as "I embrace the enduring power of agape love, navigating life's complexities with resilience, compassion, and understanding."

_____

_____

_____

_____

_____

- Repeat: Recite this affirmation daily to reinforce your dedication to practicing and embodying agape love in your relationships.

_____

_____

_____

_____

_____

7. Reflection on Progress

- Monitor: At the end of each week, review how your understanding and practice of agape love have evolved. How has this affected your relationships and ability to navigate love amid complexities?

_____

_____

_____

_____

_____

- Adjust: Consider any adjustments needed in your approach to love and relationships. What new steps can you take to deepen your practice of agape love?

_____

_____

_____

_____

_____

Chapter on Marriage

Deep Reflections

- Prompt: Reflecting on the symphony of love and self-discovery within marriage, how do you perceive the interplay between honoring the sanctity of union and embracing individual completeness? Drawing from the lessons of resilience, understanding, and unwavering strength, how do you navigate the journey of marriage as a tapestry uniquely woven with shared experiences and personal growth? Moreover, when considering the tempo of connection, how do you balance patience to allow for harmonious alignment with the desire for fulfillment, recognizing that the most beautiful symphonies are composed of perfectly tuned notes, not rushed improvisations?

Scriptural Foundations

- Matrimonial Chronicles (Hebrews 13:4): "Marriage should be honored by all, and the marriage bed kept pure, for God will judge the adulterer and all the sexually immoral." Reflect on how this scripture emphasizes the sanctity and respect of marriage, encouraging faithfulness and integrity within the union.
- Harmony in the Broken Symphony (James 4:1–3): "What causes fights and quarrels among you? Don't they come from your desires that battle within you? You desire but do not have, so you kill. You covet but you cannot get what you want, so you quarrel and fight. You do not have because you do not ask God. When you ask, you do not receive, because you ask with wrong motives, that you may spend what you get on your pleasures." Contemplate how this scripture addresses the conflicts that can arise in relationships and the importance of seeking harmony by aligning desires with divine will.

Actionable Steps

1. Honoring Union and Embracing Individuality

- Reflect: Contemplate how you balance honoring the sanctity of marriage with maintaining your sense of individual completeness. How do you honor both the union and your personal growth?

_____

_____

_____

_____

_____

_____

_____

- Write: Describe a specific example where you successfully navigated the balance between togetherness and individuality in your marriage. How did this experience affect your relationship?

_____

_____

_____

_____

_____

_____

_____

2. Journaling Exercise

- Explore: Write about how resilience, understanding, and unwavering strength play a role in your marriage. How have these qualities helped you navigate challenges and grow together?

_____

_____

_____

_____

_____

- Contemplate: Reflect on your personal growth within the marriage. How has your journey of self-discovery influenced your relationship?

_____

_____

_____

_____

_____

3. Navigating Shared Experiences and Growth

- Identify: Identify key shared experiences that have shaped your marriage. How do these experiences contribute to the tapestry of your relationship?

_____

_____

_____

_____

_____

- Act: Develop a plan for continuing to weave new shared experiences into your marriage while also nurturing your personal growth. What steps can you take to enrich your journey together?

4. Balancing Connection and Fulfillment

- Reflect: Consider how you balance the desire for fulfillment with the need for patience in your marriage. How does this balance affect the harmony and growth of your relationship?

_____

_____

_____

_____

_____

_____

_____

- Document: Write about how you manage the tempo of connection and patience. How does this approach contribute to a harmonious and fulfilling relationship?

_____

_____

_____

_____

_____

_____

_____

5. Creating a Symphony of Marriage

- Visualize: Imagine your marriage as a symphony, with each partner contributing unique notes to the composition. How do you ensure that the symphony is composed of perfectly tuned notes rather than rushed improvisations?

_____

_____

_____

_____

_____

- Illustrate: Create a visual or written representation of how you and your partner contribute to this symphony. How do you work together to achieve harmony and fulfillment?

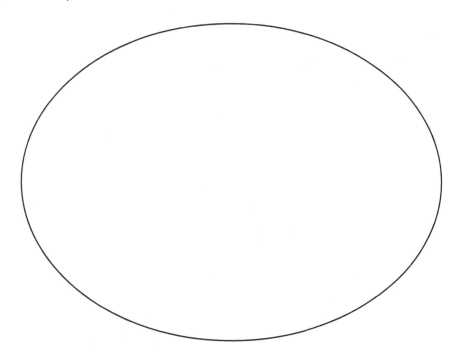

6. Daily Affirmation

- Write: Craft an affirmation that reflects your commitment to both honoring the sanctity of your union and embracing personal growth, such as "I honor the sacred bond of marriage while nurturing my individual growth, creating a harmonious symphony through patience and understanding."

_____

_____

_____

_____

_____

- Repeat: Recite this affirmation daily to reinforce your dedication to balancing connection and personal fulfillment within your marriage.

_____

_____

_____

_____

_____

7. Reflection on Progress

- Monitor: At the end of each week, review how your understanding and practice of balancing union and individuality have evolved. How has this affected the harmony and growth in your marriage?

_____

_____

_____

_____

_____

- Adjust: Consider any adjustments needed in your approach to balancing connection and personal fulfillment. What new steps can you take to continue enriching your marriage?

_____

_____

_____

_____

_____

Chapter on Balance

Deep Reflections

- Prompt: Reflecting on the allure and dangers of gambling or other vices, what steps can you take to resist the temptation of easy riches and instead cultivate a sense of fulfillment and contentment with your life? Contemplating the dance of life illuminated by Ecclesiastes, how do you establish boundaries and prioritize the rhythm of your personal and professional spheres to achieve a harmonious blend? Considering the beauty of balance and the joy of shared moments, how do you navigate the seasons of life, recognizing that each holds its unique dance? Moreover, as you pedal toward liberation and embrace the twists and turns of your journey, how do you unveil the extraordinary resilience within, finding the rhythm that resonates with your heart amid the symphony of life?

Scriptural Foundations

- Navigating the Tightrope of Wealth and Temptation (1 Timothy 6:9–10): "Those who want to get rich fall into temptation and a trap and into many foolish and harmful desires that plunge people into ruin and destruction. For the love of money is a root of all kinds of evil. Some people, eager for money, have wandered from the faith and pierced themselves with many griefs." Reflect on how this scripture encourages us to maintain a balanced perspective on material wealth, understanding the dangers of allowing the pursuit of riches to overshadow spiritual values.
- Navigating Work and Life Harmony (Ecclesiastes 3:1): "There is a time for everything, and a season for every activity under the heavens." Contemplate how this scripture speaks to the importance

of achieving harmony in different aspects of life by recognizing that each has its own season and rightful place.

- A Journey Home to Self-Discovery (James 1:22–25): "Do not merely listen to the word, and so deceive yourselves. Do what it says. Anyone who listens to the word but does not do what it says is like someone who looks at his face in a mirror and, after looking at himself, goes away and immediately forgets what he looks like. But whoever looks intently into the perfect law that gives freedom, and continues in it—not forgetting what they have heard, but doing it—they will be blessed in what they do." Reflect on how this scripture encourages aligning your actions with your beliefs, promoting a balance between self-awareness and purposeful living.

Actionable Steps

1. Resisting Temptations and Cultivating Fulfillment

- Reflect: Contemplate the allure of gambling or other vices and how they promise easy riches. What temptations have you faced, and how have they affected your sense of fulfillment?

_____

_____

_____

_____

_____

_____

_____

_____

- Write: Describe the steps you can take to resist these temptations and instead cultivate contentment in your life. What strategies can you implement to enhance your sense of fulfillment?

_____

_____

_____

_____

_____

_____

2. Journaling Exercise

- Explore: Write about how you can apply the wisdom from Ecclesiastes to establish boundaries between personal and professional life. How do you plan to prioritize and maintain a harmonious blend?

_____

_____

_____

_____

_____

_____

- Contemplate: Reflect on the rhythm of your life and how you can create a balanced approach to managing your responsibilities and passions.

_____

_____

_____

_____

_____

3. Establishing Boundaries and Prioritizing Rhythm

- Identify: Identify specific areas where boundaries are needed to achieve a better balance between personal and professional spheres. What steps will you take to set and maintain these boundaries?

_____

_____

_____

_____

_____

- Act: Develop a plan for prioritizing your responsibilities and activities to maintain a harmonious rhythm in your life. How will you ensure that each sphere of your life gets the attention it needs?

_____

_____

_____

_____

_____

4. Navigating Life's Seasons

- Reflect: Consider the different seasons of your life and how each one offers its own unique dance. How do you adapt to these changes and find joy in each phase?

_____

_____

_____

_____

_____

- Document: Write about how you navigate the transitions between different seasons and how you embrace the beauty of each stage.

_____

_____

_____

_____

_____

_____

_____

_____

5. Unveiling Resilience and Finding Rhythm

- Explore: Reflect on the extraordinary resilience within you as you navigate the twists and turns of your journey. How do you find the rhythm that resonates with your heart amid life's challenges?

_____

_____

_____

_____

_____

_____

_____

_____

- Illustrate: Create a visual or written representation of your journey toward liberation and balance. How does this rhythm align with your personal values and goals?

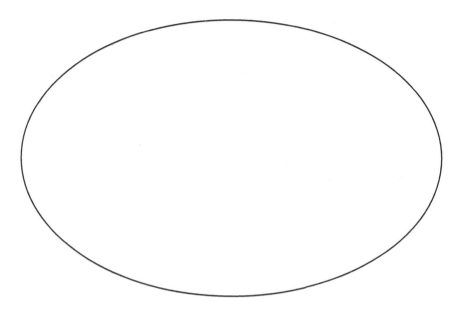

6. Daily Affirmation

- Write: Craft an affirmation that reflects your commitment to resisting temptations, establishing boundaries, and embracing balance, such as "I cultivate fulfillment and contentment by resisting temptation, establishing harmonious boundaries, and embracing the unique rhythm of each season of life."

_____

_____

_____

_____

_____

- Repeat: Recite this affirmation daily to reinforce your dedication to maintaining balance and resilience in your life.

_____

_____

_____

_____

_____

7. Reflection on Progress

- Monitor: At the end of each week, review how your understanding and practice of balance have evolved. How has this affected your sense of fulfillment and harmony?

_____

_____

_____

_____

_____

- Adjust: Consider any adjustments needed in your approach to achieving balance. What new steps can you take to continue refining your sense of rhythm and resilience?

_____

_____

_____

_____

_____

Chapter on Grief

Deep Reflections

- Prompt: Reflecting on the roller coaster of life and the inevitability of mourning, how do you navigate grief amid unexpected moments of laughter and joy? Considering the comforting light that guides us through the shadows, how do you embrace the ride of life while acknowledging the pain of loss? Moreover, in the pursuit of light as a constant companion, how do you find solace and resilience amid the twists and turns of grief's journey?

Scriptural Foundations

- Shadows of Loss (Matthew 5:4): "Blessed are those who mourn, for they will be comforted." Reflect on how this scripture offers solace in times of grief, reminding us that comfort and peace are promised to those who mourn. Consider how this divine comfort can help you honor the memory of loved ones and find peace in their legacy, even through the pain of loss.
- Silent Wounds (Psalm 34:18): "The Lord is close to the brokenhearted and saves those who are crushed in spirit." This verse speaks to the deep, often invisible wounds we carry in times of loss. It reminds us that even in our silent suffering, God draws near, offering healing to our crushed spirits. Reflect on how this scripture can guide you through the quiet pain of grief, reassuring you that even when words fail, divine support is ever-present, holding you in moments of vulnerability and helping you find strength in the midst of silent wounds.

Actionable Steps

1. Navigating Grief amid Joy

- Reflect: Contemplate how grief and moments of joy coexist in your life. How do you navigate the complex emotions of mourning while still experiencing laughter and happiness?

_____

_____

_____

_____

_____

- Write: Describe a situation where you experienced grief alongside moments of joy. How did you manage these conflicting emotions, and what insights did you gain from this experience?

_____

_____

_____

_____

_____

_____

2. Journaling Exercise

- Explore: Write about how the inevitability of mourning affects your daily life. How do you balance acknowledging the pain of loss with embracing moments of joy?

_____

_____

_____

_____

_____

- Contemplate: Reflect on how you can allow yourself to experience both grief and joy without feeling conflicted. What practices help you integrate these emotions into your life?

_____

_____

_____

_____

_____

3. Embracing Life's Ride

- Identify: Identify ways in which you can embrace the ride of life, even as you face the pain of loss. How can you acknowledge and honor your grief while continuing to engage with life's experiences?

_____

_____

_____

_____

- Act: Develop a plan for incorporating practices that help you remain engaged with life's joys and challenges while navigating grief. What steps can you take to find balance?

_____

_____

_____

_____

_____

4. Finding Solace and Resilience

- Reflect: Consider the comforting light that guides you through the shadows of grief. How do you find solace and resilience amid the challenges of mourning?

_____

_____

_____

_____

_____

- Document: Write about sources of comfort and strength that help you navigate the twists and turns of grief. How do these sources support your journey?

_____

_____

_____

_____

_____

_____

5. Pursuit of Light and Resilience

- Explore: Reflect on how the pursuit of light, or hope and positivity, serves as a constant companion in your journey through grief. How does this light guide you through the darker moments?

_____

_____

_____

_____

_____

_____

- Illustrate: Create a visual or written representation of how you seek and find light amid your grief. How does this pursuit influence your ability to cope and heal?

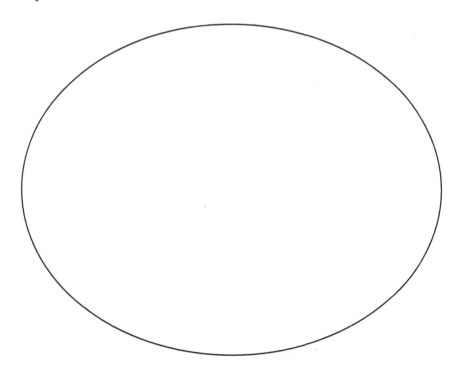

6. Daily Affirmation

- Write: Craft an affirmation that reflects your commitment to finding balance between grief and joy and seeking solace and resilience, such as "I navigate the roller coaster of life with grace, embracing both grief and joy while finding comfort and resilience in the light that guides me."

_____

_____

_____

_____

_____

- Repeat: Recite this affirmation daily to reinforce your dedication to balancing grief with moments of joy and seeking solace in the journey.

_____

_____

_____

_____

_____

7. Reflection on Progress

- Monitor: At the end of each week, review how your understanding and practice of navigating grief have evolved. How has this affected your ability to find joy and solace amid mourning?

_____

_____

_____

_____

_____

- Adjust: Consider any adjustments needed in your approach to dealing with grief. What new steps can you take to continue finding resilience and light in your journey?

_____

_____

_____

_____

_____

_____

Chapter on Finding Home

Deep Reflections

- Prompt: Reflecting on the journey through the vivid colors of cultural embroidery woven into your story, how do you define the concept of *home* beyond its physical boundaries? Considering the lesson that home is not just a place but a feeling, how do you navigate the exploration and connection to the myriad homes awaiting in the vast expanse of the world? Moreover, how do you find inspiration in transcending borders to discover the true essence of home within yourself and the connections you cultivate?

Scriptural Foundations

- Beyond Borders: Discovering My Forever Home (Psalm 127:1): "Unless the Lord builds the house, the builders labor in vain. Unless the Lord watches over the city, the guards stand watch in vain." Reflect on how this verse informs your understanding of home as more than just a physical space, emphasizing the importance of divine presence and guidance in building a true sense of belonging.

Actionable Steps

1. Defining Home beyond Physical Boundaries

- Reflect: Contemplate what *home* means to you beyond just a physical space. How do you experience *home* through your cultural, emotional, and relational connections?

_____

_____

_____

_____

- Write: Describe how your understanding of *home* has evolved over time. What aspects of your journey have contributed to this broader definition?

_____

_____

_____

_____

_____

_____

2. Journaling Exercise

- Explore: Write about different places or experiences where you have felt a strong sense of home. How did these experiences shape your view of what constitutes *home*?

_____

_____

_____

_____

_____

- Contemplate: Reflect on how the concept of home as a feeling rather than a place influences your daily life and relationships.

_____

_____

_____

_____

_____

_____

3. Navigating Exploration and Connection

- Identify: Identify the various homes you have encountered in your life, whether cultural, emotional, or relational. How do these experiences contribute to your understanding of *home*?

_____

_____

_____

_____

_____

- Act: Develop a plan for exploring and connecting with new homes or communities. How can you cultivate meaningful connections that align with your sense of home?

_____

_____

_____

_____

_____

4. Finding Inspiration in Transcending Borders

- Reflect: Consider how transcending physical and cultural borders has helped you discover the essence of home within yourself. How does this expanded perspective influence your sense of belonging?

_____

_____

_____

_____

- Document: Write about instances where crossing borders—whether literal or metaphorical—has led to new insights about home. How has this inspired you to connect more deeply with yourself and others?

_____

_____

_____

_____

_____

_____

5.   Discovering the Essence of Home

- Explore: Reflect on how you can find and nurture the essence of home within yourself. What practices or habits help you cultivate a sense of belonging and comfort, regardless of your location?

_____

_____

_____

_____

_____

- Illustrate: Create a visual or written representation of the elements that contribute to your sense of home. How do these elements help you feel grounded and connected?

_____

_____

_____

_____

_____

6.   Daily Affirmation

- Write: Craft an affirmation that reflects your journey in discovering and nurturing the true essence of home, such as "I find and create a sense of home through the connections I cultivate, the cultural richness I embrace, and the essence I carry within myself."

_____

_____

_____

_____

_____

- Repeat: Recite this affirmation daily to reinforce your commitment to exploring and cultivating a profound sense of home.

_____

_____

_____

_____

_____

7.   Reflection on Progress
- Monitor: At the end of each week, review how your understanding and experience of *home* have evolved. How has this affected your sense of belonging and connection?

_____

_____

_____

_____

_____

- Adjust: Consider any adjustments needed in your approach to finding and nurturing *home*. What new steps can you take to deepen your connection to this concept?

_____

_____

_____

_____

_____

Chapter on Peace

Deep Reflections

- Prompt: Reflecting on the transition to a slower pace and embracing retirement as an uncharted adventure, how do you find peace in trusting the future and seeking divine guidance, as illuminated by Numbers 8:23–24? Considering the symphony of practices that resonate with your soul, how do you craft intentional movements that harmonize with the essence of your being, creating a masterpiece of peace in each step? Moreover, how do you perceive the profound beauty in life's dance with peace, recognizing that it's not just about the destination but the journey itself?

Scriptural Foundations

- From Dying to Live to Living to Die (Ecclesiastes 9:10): "Whatever your hand finds to do, do it with all your might, for in the realm of the dead, where you are going, there is neither working nor planning nor knowledge nor wisdom." Reflect on how this verse inspires you to live fully and with purpose in each moment, fostering peace through purposeful action.
- Retirement and Rediscovery (Numbers 8:23–24): "The Lord said to Moses, 'This applies to the Levites: Men twenty-five years old or more shall come to take part in the work at the tent of meeting, but at the age of fifty, they must retire from their regular service and work no longer.'" Consider how this scripture guides your understanding of retirement as a time for rediscovery and peace, trusting in divine timing and purpose.
- Nurturing Peace (Philippians 4:7): "And the peace of God, which transcends all understanding, will guard your hearts and your minds in Christ Jesus." Reflect on how this verse shapes your approach to nurturing inner peace, allowing divine peace to guide and protect you.

Actionable Steps

1. Finding Peace in Trusting the Future

- Reflect: Consider how the transition to a slower pace or retirement is a new adventure. How do you find peace in trusting that this phase of life holds opportunities for growth and divine guidance?

_____

_____

_____

_____

_____

- Write: Describe your feelings about this transition. How do you seek divine guidance, and how does Numbers 8:23–24 inspire you to trust the future?

_____

_____

_____

_____

_____

2. Journaling Exercise

- Explore: Write about the practices and rituals that resonate with your soul and contribute to your sense of peace. How do these practices help you create harmony and balance in your life?

_____

_____

_____

_____

- Contemplate: Reflect on how you can integrate these practices into your daily routine to enhance your sense of inner peace.

_____

_____

_____

_____

_____

_____

3.   Crafting Intentional Movements

- Identify: Identify specific actions or changes you can make to align with your essence and create peace in your life. What intentional movements can you adopt to harmonize with your inner self?

_____

_____

_____

_____

_____

- Act: Develop a plan for implementing these intentional movements. How can you incorporate them into your daily life to create a masterpiece of peace?

_____

_____

_____

_____

_____

4. Perceiving the Beauty in Life's Dance with Peace

- Reflect: Contemplate the concept of peace as a dance rather than a destination. How do you experience the beauty in the journey of finding peace, rather than focusing solely on the end goal?

_____

_____

_____

_____

_____

- Document: Write about moments in your life when you have felt at peace. How does this understanding of peace as a dance influence your perspective and approach to life's journey?

_____

_____

_____

_____

_____

5. Embracing the Journey

- Explore: Reflect on how embracing the journey, with its ups and downs, contributes to a deeper sense of peace. How can you appreciate the process and the growth that comes with each step of your journey?

_____

_____

_____

_____

_____

- Illustrate: Create a visual or written representation of your journey toward peace. How does this imagery help you see the beauty in the process?

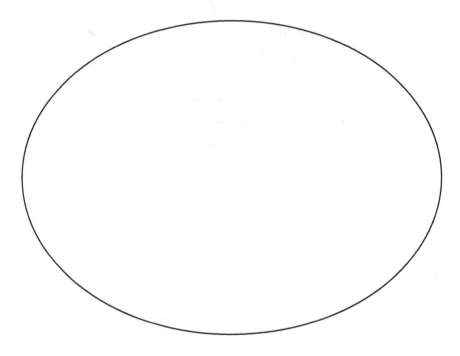

6. Daily Affirmation

- Write: Craft an affirmation that reflects your commitment to finding and nurturing peace through trust, intentionality, and appreciation of the journey, such as "I embrace the journey of life with peace, trusting in divine guidance and crafting intentional movements that harmonize with my essence."

_____

_____

_____

_____

_____

_____

- Repeat: Recite this affirmation daily to reinforce your dedication to finding and creating peace in your life.

_____

_____

_____

_____

_____

7. Reflection on Progress

- Monitor: At the end of each week, review how your sense of peace has evolved. How has your approach to embracing the journey and trusting the future influenced your overall peace of mind?

_____

_____

_____

_____

_____

- Adjust: Consider any adjustments needed in your practices or perspective. What new steps can you take to further enhance your sense of peace?

_____

_____

_____

_____

_____

Scripture References

Faith

- Isaiah 40:8 (NIV): "The grass withers and the flowers fall, but the word of our God endures forever."
- Proverbs 3:5–6 (NIV): "Trust in the Lord with all your heart and lean not on your own understanding; in all your ways submit to him, and he will make your paths straight."
- Exodus 15:2 (NIV): "The Lord is my strength and my defense; he has become my salvation. He is my God, and I will praise him, my father's God, and I will exalt him."

Identity

- Ezekiel 36:26 (NIV): "I will give you a new heart and put a new spirit in you; I will remove from you your heart of stone and give you a heart of flesh."
- Psalm 119:105 (NIV): "Your word is a lamp to my feet and a light for my path."
- Galatians 3:28 (NIV): "There is neither Jew nor Gentile, neither slave nor free, neither male nor female, for you are all one in Christ Jesus."

Solitude

- 1 Corinthians 16:13–14 (NIV): "Be on your guard; stand firm in the faith; be courageous; be strong. Do everything in love."
- Jeremiah 29:11–13 (NIV): "'For I know the plans I have for you,' declares the Lord, 'plans to prosper you and not to harm you, plans to give you hope and a future. Then you will call on me and come

and pray to me, and I will listen to you. You will seek me and find me when you seek me with all your heart.'"

- Psalm 143 (NIV): "Lord, hear my prayer, listen to my cry for mercy; in your faithfulness and righteousness come to my relief."

Transformation

- Romans 12:2 (NIV): "Do not conform to the pattern of this world, but be transformed by the renewing of your mind. Then you will be able to test and approve what God's will is—his good, pleasing and perfect will."
- 1 Timothy 3:1–7 (NIV): "Here is a trustworthy saying: Whoever aspires to be an overseer desires a noble task. Now the overseer is to be above reproach, faithful to his wife, temperate, self-controlled, respectable, hospitable, able to teach, not given to drunkenness, not violent but gentle, not quarrelsome, not a lover of money."
- Isaiah 55:11 (NIV): "So is my word that goes out from my mouth: It will not return to me empty, but will accomplish what I desire and achieve the purpose for which I sent it."

Purpose

- Romans 8:28 (NIV): "And we know that in all things God works for the good of those who love him, who have been called according to his purpose."
- Proverbs 16:3 (NIV): "Commit to the Lord whatever you do, and he will establish your plans."
- James 1:12–14 (NIV): "Blessed is the one who perseveres under trial because, having stood the test, that person will receive the crown of life that the Lord has promised to those who love him. When tempted, no one should say, 'God is tempting me.' For God cannot be tempted by evil, nor does he tempt anyone; but each

person is tempted when they are dragged away by their own evil desire and enticed."

Freedom

- Colossians 3:21 (NIV): "Fathers, do not embitter your children, or they will become discouraged."
- Ezekiel 7:10 (NIV): "The day is here! It has come! Doom has burst forth, the rod has budded, arrogance has blossomed!"
- 1 John 4:8 (NIV): "Whoever does not love does not know God, because God is love."

Gifts

- Matthew 2:10–11 (NIV): "When they saw the star, they were overjoyed. On coming to the house, they saw the child with his mother Mary, and they bowed down and worshiped him. Then they opened their treasures and presented him with gifts of gold, frankincense and myrrh."
- Psalm 127:3 (NIV): "Children are a heritage from the Lord, offspring a reward from him."

Love

- Matthew 5:44 (NIV): "But I tell you, love your enemies and pray for those who persecute you."
- 1 Corinthians 16:14 (NIV): "Do everything in love."

Marriage

- Hebrews 13:4 (NIV): "Marriage should be honored by all, and the marriage bed kept pure, for God will judge the adulterer and all the sexually immoral."

- James 4:1–3 (NIV): "What causes fights and quarrels among you? Don't they come from your desires that battle within you? You desire but do not have, so you kill. You covet but you cannot get what you want, so you quarrel and fight. You do not have because you do not ask God. When you ask, you do not receive, because you ask with wrong motives, that you may spend what you get on your pleasures."

Balance

- 1 Timothy 6:9–10 (NIV): "Those who want to get rich fall into temptation and a trap and into many foolish and harmful desires that plunge people into ruin and destruction. For the love of money is a root of all kinds of evil. Some people, eager for money, have wandered from the faith and pierced themselves with many griefs."
- Ecclesiastes 3:1 (NIV): "There is a time for everything, and a season for every activity under the heavens."
- James 1:22–25 (NIV): "Do not merely listen to the word, and so deceive yourselves. Do what it says. Anyone who listens to the word but does not do what it says is like someone who looks at his face in a mirror and, after looking at himself, goes away and immediately forgets what he looks like. But whoever looks intently into the perfect law that gives freedom, and continues in it—not forgetting what they have heard, but doing it—they will be blessed in what they do."

Grief

- Matthew 5:4 (NIV): "Blessed are those who mourn, for they will be comforted."

- Psalm 34:18 (NIV): "The Lord is close to the brokenhearted and saves those who are crushed in spirit."

Finding Home

- Psalm 127:1 (NIV): "Unless the Lord builds the house, the builders labor in vain. Unless the Lord watches over the city, the guards stand watch in vain."

Peace

- Numbers 8:23–24 (NIV): "The Lord said to Moses, 'This is what applies to the Levites: Men twenty-five years old or more shall come to take part in the work at the tent of meeting. But at the age of fifty, they must retire from their regular service and work no longer.'"
- Ecclesiastes 9:10 (NIV): "Whatever your hand finds to do, do it with all your might, for in the realm of the dead, where you are going, there is neither working nor planning nor knowledge nor wisdom."
- Philippians 4:7 (NIV): "And the peace of God, which transcends all understanding, will guard your hearts and your minds in Christ Jesus."

Printed in the United States
by Baker & Taylor Publisher Services